ALIEN

EXAMINING JESUS CHRIST IN A UFO UNIVERSE

JEFF BENNINGTON

ALIEN

Examining Jesus Christ in a UFO Universe

Jeff Bennington

Published by Nexgate Press

COPYRIGHT

Published by Nexgate Press, 2014.
ISBN-13: 978-1499285130
ISBN-10: 1499285132

TABLE OF CONTENTS

INTRODUCTION

"For our struggle is not against flesh and blood, but against the rulers, against the authorities, against the powers of this dark world and against the spiritual forces of evil in the heavenly realms." ~ Ephesians 6:12

Millions of people around the world are trying to make sense of what appears to be an active UFO universe. What seems to be going on is testing our belief systems and causing an explosion of interest in the UFO phenomenon. The excitement has reached epic proportions, stirring the interest of web surfers, UFO enthusiasts, and big name celebrities like mega-selling pop star, Katy Perry, who said in a June 2011 Rolling Stone interview that she is "obsessed" with the History Channel's Ancient Alien program. In regard to the show's ancient alien theory, Perry said, "It all seems to connect the dots. It's blowing my mind."[a]

Millions have tuned in to the Ancient Alien broadcast since 2010 and despite the fact that many view the programming as pseudo-science, the philosophical impact of their premise—that humans are descendants from a distant alien race—is quite significant, inspiring an ever-growing cult culture. In a country dominated by a Judeo-Christian faith, it would appear that such ideologies would fade into the cable-network sunset within a season or two, but that is not the case. The program has run six seasons and is still going strong at the time of this writing, not because the ideas are so solid in their support and research, but because the UFO phenomenon is so real to so many people. And these people are looking for answers. Many are wondering if we were created by God, and UFOs and alien abductions are a real phenomenon, who exactly is God? Is God completely different from what we were told? Is God actually a benevolent alien race? If so, what does this mean to our lives, our beliefs, and the human destiny? Are we loved by a divine entity, or are we nothing more than a cosmic DNA experiment?

These are the claims of some ancient astronaut theorists. But do they stand up against the facts? Can their evidence be trusted? Are they on to something, or is their premise faulted? Whatever the case may be, I hope to clarify these questions and take the answers one step further into the celestial realm.

Despite the believability or un-believability of the UFO phenomenon, thousands of eyewitnesses come forward every year, including high-level military and governmental officials. But this book is not about proving the existence of UFOs or extraterrestrials. This book was constructed to examine the philosophical and spiritual implications of a UFO presence here on earth. Thus the driving force behind this book—how to make sense of Jesus Christ in a UFO universe.

~†~

Because of my personal interest in this topic, I didn't actually write this book for you; I wrote it for myself. Still, I hope that you find some value in the pages to come. I've spent countless hours reading and studying, but like any work on this subject, I admit that what follows is strictly my opinion.

Before we begin, you should know that this book started to germinate while I was writing a series of thriller novels I started in 2010 and was sure to wrap up long before 2014. Unfortunately, there was a problem. The series required me to dig deeper into the UFO phenomenon than I had expected, which at the time was limited to Wikipedia and cable programming. To better equip my pages with alien mysteries, I spent hundreds of hours researching the maze of deep underground military bases, and reading the vast tales of ancient alien theories, examining UFO encounters and abduction accounts. In doing so, I found myself digging one rabbit hole after another, growing dizzy as I spiraled deeper into the abyss. The stories I uncovered were stranger than fiction and provided a slew of book ideas ranging from alien controlled governments to genetic warfare between earth and distant planets. Yet no matter how bizarre the tales, the overriding premise in all of my findings was that something is really going on. Despite the outlandish conspiracy theories and clashing opinions in the field, the evidence seemed to agree with one truth: we have and continue to be visited by strangers from beyond this place we call earth. And yet we are not even close to resolving who or what they are.

Theories abound, and the many contradictions on the subject made my research all the more difficult. Who's right? Who's wrong? What are the facts? Is anyone really impartial? I needed to know the truth, and I needed to know sooner rather than later. But the deeper I found myself in the muck and mire of these seemingly "solved" mysteries, the more questions I had.

I've written several books that deal with supernatural topics, so I was quite familiar with the paranormal realm. I've imagined the impossible, the unthinkable, the surreal and grotesque, and yet whatever is going on is as much psychic as any fictional yarn I've penned. I dug through book after book on the subject until one day I found myself immersed in a volume about ancient Mesopotamian religions; that's when I finally hit rock bottom. I mean, who wants to study Mesopotamian history? But that's where I landed, and that's what it took for the story of our UFO universe to unfold, for me to make sense of it all.

After digging up everything I found on the subject, it was easy to imagine the picture I had painted with the colors of my research to be the final answer, but I knew better. Everyone has an opinion; and who am I? At the very least I had hoped to add a sliver of truth to the other contributions that have been published on this subject. And so I say this as humbly as I possibly can—I believe this book is a much-needed resource for me, if not for anyone else.

I truly could not continue writing fiction until I resolved the UFO issue for myself because I spent so much time considering the consequences of an alien existence, that I felt like I was in a literary chokehold. The possibilities offset my point of reference as a writer, as a human, leaving me to doubt my belief system, and shaking my personal compass. How could I continue to interject themes about life, and flavor my writing with ideas that no longer made sense in the presence of a UFO universe, ideas that no longer made sense to me? I didn't want to look stupid—a fear that I've been lugging around for years.

I probably took all of this a little too far, a little too seriously, and should have just kept on writing with my feet on the ground regardless of what people say about UFOs and extraterrestrials. But I couldn't do that. I felt compelled to continue my quest. As a result I was growing increasingly lost.

What was the problem?

The problem was that I needed to understand how and if Jesus Christ fits into our UFO universe—not for my series— for me on a personal, on a spiritual level. Although I'm ashamed to admit it, I was thoroughly convinced that the ancient astronaut theorists had the answers to human existence and our origins here on earth, believing that UFOs and their pilots could be associated with our histories and human origin. Their televised arguments were compelling, and the imagery and sound bites made perfect sense at the time. When I opened the books the ancient alien theorists referenced, I found, for the most part, that the bullet points from their research were generally correct. Consequently, I'd tune in the following week to hear more of their titillating declarations as if I had been born again in the First Church of the Alien Brotherhood, hanging on their every word.

My near-baptism in the ancient alien religion was shocking my faith to say the least. I was pulled into the cult— hook, line and sinker. Fortunately, I had enough sense to begin writing this book with an open mind; open to evidence even if it contradicted my Judeo-Christian worldview, which is actually what I expected to find. And that's what happened on the front end. But somewhere in the middle I began to discover holes in the ancient astronaut theories, contradictions in the alien agenda, but most importantly similarities in the UFO phenomenon that aligned with scripture.

As a result, you are reading the second version of this book. The first endeavored to confirm that Jesus Christ was an alien from a distant planet (Heaven), and that his uniqueness was due to his higher spirituality. The second book—the book you're reading now—is my ultimate conclusion in the loosest sense of the word. Although I began writing this with a completely different premise, nearing the doorstep of my dying faith, the evidence brought me full circle, causing me to delete tens of thousands of words, and seeing Jesus Christ as the King of Kings in a way I had never imagined, nor expected in a world where UFOs are increasingly abuzz.

Does this mean I no longer believe in the existence of UFOs or the possibility of alien life elsewhere in the cosmos? Not at all. That would be irrelevant anyway. Who am I to make such a declaration? I'm just a writer, and this book is just my theory. And my theory is that Jesus of Nazareth fits square in the middle of this place teeming with unidentified flying objects and ancient aerial battles in the heavens. Jesus Christ, in my opinion, is the Admiral of the biggest UFO fleet man will ever see.

So as we investigate together, you should be warned that clawing our way through the initial mound of information is daunting and necessary, but once we break through the preliminary information, you will begin to see the Bible in a different light—I did anyway. And although I cannot presume to know what you believe, I do hope you see Jesus Christ differently, too.

1.

SUPERNATURAL

One of the greatest mysteries in the Bible is found in a very simple passage stating that the woman's seed would relentlessly contend with the seed of the serpent. The passage in Genesis 3:15 poses so many questions that its density is off the charts, bursting at the seams with strangeness and spiritual implications. The verse is simply written,

"And I will put enmity between you and the woman, and between your offspring [seed] and hers; he will crush your head, and you will strike his heel."

Although the Messianic insinuations are dismissed by most Jewish doctrines, many Christians believe this verse is the first prophetic passage concerning the seed of the Messiah as it relates to a spiritual battle between the serpent and the woman's offspring. This prophecy was fleshed out in Mel Gibson's, *The Passion of the Christ*. In the opening scene, Jesus was praying in the garden as Satan watched over him. Then just before Jesus stood up to rebuke his sleepy friends, a snake slithered near the Savior's feet. When Jesus took a step forward, he crushed the serpent's head, suggesting that what was about to occur would satisfy the prophecy.

According to scripture, the battle commenced in the heavens with Lucifer's rebellion, and as promised, will come to an end in the Clouds when Christ returns with thousands of his angels. The war did not begin with a swing of the sword or a blow to the skull; it began with a lie, a spiritually deadly blow that still echoes in the hearts of all mankind, and still looming in our UFO universe.

There are differing ideas about who and what the serpent was. Whether the serpent was an instrument used by Satan, possessed by, a member of a reptilian race, or the embodiment of Satan himself, is not the point. God promised that a battle would persist between the woman and the serpent's seed because of the rebellion that took place. And from that day forward, everything changed.

The battle over the "seed" would rage over the course of thousands of years, carrying the Hebrew nation through the desert and into the Promised Land despite enslavement and captivity that lasted for centuries. Their ultimate redemption was made possible not by military might, luck, or great numbers, but rather by multiple supernatural occurrences, and angelic intervention. The many battles fought were between powerful kingdoms, giants, and the Nephilim, a mysterious race that still confounds biblical scholars. In the face of constant turmoil, the Israelites would carry the Messianic seed approximately 4,000 years, through barren women and faithful fathers, until a roving "star" finally guided it over Bethlehem, birthed by the Virgin Mary, and celebrated by angelic beings among the shepherds.

Thirty years after the birth of the Christ child, we find Jesus fasting in the desert. The air is balmy and the wind is fierce as the sojourner embarks upon his spiritual quest. His sandals are worn and his lips are dry and cracked from the relentless sun. The man has lived a life bathed in prophecy and mystery predating his birth, and here he was preparing himself to turn much of the world upside down. Hundreds of prophecies pointed to this Hebrew who would rise from the priestly tribe of Levi and from the royal line of King David. I can only imagine the weight bearing down upon his shoulders, as he perceived his coming ministry, trial, and execution.

When Jesus was nearly exhausted from his forty-day fast, a powerful creature confronted him with sinister intentions. The devil—a fallen angel—had come to test this "Son of Man", the so-called Messiah. Where the devil was before or after this episode, we can only guess. And yet the scene implicates that prophetic statement made in the beginning... *he will crush your head, and you will strike his heel...* assuring the reader that the conflict continued to that very day when these two warriors met head on.

One prepared for battle, clothed in prayer, and armed with God's word.

The other scrutinized his opponent, checking for weaknesses, examining the Son of Man's level of commitment and discipline.

Although many years had passed since the Genesis 3:15 declaration, Satan made Jesus an offer. Interestingly it had nothing to do with knowledge, or the ability to be *like God*— perhaps because Satan knew exactly whom he was talking to.

This time the deceiver presented food, wealth, and power. In this angelic encounter, the devil suggests that Jesus turn the rocks into bread, that is, if he was the Son of God. Jesus averted the deceiver's trap by quoting scripture. Then by means of flight or a powerful vision, Satan carried the Hebrew to the highest point of Israel's temple. The devil proposed that Jesus jump from the temple to show his authority over God's angels, allowing the priests and all who were present to witness the angels catching his fall. Although that must have been a tempting offer, Jesus declined once again. In response, Satan carried Jesus along in a whirlwind showing him the kingdoms of the world and offered them to the poor, hungry carpenter. Jesus declined a third time, overcoming the evil one, victorious in his first terrestrial encounter with a fallen angel.

"Then Jesus was led by the Spirit into the wilderness to be tempted by the devil. After fasting forty days and forty nights, he was hungry. The tempter came to him and said, "If you are the Son of God, tell these stones to become bread." Jesus answered, "It is written: 'Man shall not live on bread alone, but on every word that comes from the mouth of God.'"

Then the devil took him to the holy city and had him stand on the highest point of the temple. "If you are the Son of God," he said, "throw yourself down. For it is written 'He will command his angels concerning you, and they will lift you up in their hands, so that you will not strike your foot against a stone.'" Jesus answered him, "It is also written: 'Do not put the Lord your God to the test.'"

Again, the devil took him to a very high mountain and showed him all the kingdoms of the world and their splendor. "All this I will give you," he said, "if you will bow down and worship me." Jesus said to him, "Away from me, Satan! For it is written: 'Worship the Lord your God, and serve him only.'" Then the devil left him, and angels came and attended him." (Matthew 4:1-11)

In this story, Satan confronted Jesus, intent on discovering his identity and thwarting the plan of God, but the young Hebrew did not bend to the fallen angel's wishes. As a result, the devil fled and Jesus eventually walked home and began his ministry—a story you may be familiar with. But where did Satan go? According to scripture, he is still at war to dethrone God almighty and to capture the souls of men, just as he did in Genesis 3:15. Therefore, we can expect Satan and the fallen angels to continue their rebellious acts until the Messiah returns in magnificent and glorious fashion, to judge and "seize that ancient serpent, who is the devil" to bind him and throw him into the lake of burning sulfur for all eternity.

What we learn about Satan in Genesis 3:15 and his encounter with Jesus in the Matthew 4 passage, has everything to do with heaven, angels, aliens, and where Jesus fits in our UFO universe because, I believe, the UFO story begins in Genesis and ends in Revelation. To examine the UFO phenomenon between the 1940s to present does not give a complete picture. This story has begun before the gospels were written and is still being played out today. We have given the players different names and the props have changed with each new generation, but the storyline remains intact.

The words spoken by the serpent in Genesis 3:15 clearly communicate Satan's spiritual agenda—supplant God. The passage in Matthew demonstrates Satan's skill at generating powerful, psychological visions with supernatural, physical, and aerial or levitational elements. We know this because it's highly unlikely that Satan and Jesus actually climbed to the top of the temple or walked from the desert to scale a mountain only to walk back again. That probably would've taken another 40 days to complete that journey. There was clearly something supernatural and probably dimensional going on there.

Both stories implicate Lucifer, Satan, or the devil—the leader of a spiritual rebellion that took place in the heavens long before the creation of man. Both stories convey a continual spiritual pursuit to harvest the ownership of souls, or to at least turn the human soul away from God. More importantly, these stories demonstrate that the battle still rages after the rebellion in heaven, and thousands of years after the fall in the Garden of Eden.

As different as these two stories may be, they represent the same entity—evil incarnate—our adversary—the accuser—a supernatural and spiritually dimensional being capable of manifesting himself in physical form, as can the thousands of fallen angels who joined him. And this is why Genesis 3:15 is ripe with evidence of its connection with our UFO universe. Not only do we get a picture of a dimensional being so powerful that he can change his appearance to suit his deceitful strategies as we see in the creation story, we're also introduced to a creature intent on snatching human spirits from God's kingdom. In most cases, Satan does not seek his victim's physical life, because that is not necessarily what he wants. With all the knowledge and power he possesses, he simply attempted to guide Eve away from the creator by ever so slightly bending the truth. He attempted the same with Jesus to no avail.

What's interesting about Satan's tactics in these two passages is that the they are the same methods used by "aliens" today as reported by abductees and researchers—a method of control by deception, in order to change a belief system—strictly a spiritual initiative. These patterns are evident in modern alien abduction accounts, mythology, fairy-tales, and angelic encounters. Although many despise the notion that aliens are anything but extraterrestrials from other planets, the ET concept doesn't seem to fit the overriding evidence. These beings and their craft are clearly dimensional entities as evidenced by their ability to transcend our understanding of time-space. If angels possess the supernatural intelligence and powers ascribed to them in the Bible, we can only assume that their ability to transcend space-time and manipulate reality still applies today. And if the fallen angels were present here on earth long before the existence of man, could it be that they have used these thousands of years to devise a scheme that defies our imaginations?

Conceiving such a theory should not be too difficult for the believer. Our faith is built upon supernatural and paranormal possibilities. We believe in raising the dead, supernatural healing, heaven, hell, angels, demons, spirits and the Holy Ghost. Yet in light of the UFO universe, the church cringes when science interferes with our supernatural ideologies. So maybe what we thought was supernatural, is actually science fiction. Both sides cannot be right. Perhaps science is missing something by disregarding the paranormal.

Extraterrestrials and Jesus Christ cannot co-exist without both parties aware of each other. And Jesus never mentioned men from outer space. So someone is telling a lie. Thus, my first clue.

The Bible tells us that, "Eve was deceived by the serpent's cunning." (2 Corinthians 11:3). And concerning a time in the future the Apostle Paul said,

"The coming of the lawless one will be in accordance with how Satan works. He will use all sorts of displays of power through signs and wonders that serve the lie, and all the ways that wickedness deceives those who are perishing. They perish because they refused to love the truth and so be saved. **For this reason God sends them a powerful delusion so that they will believe the lie.***"* (2 Thessalonians 2:9-11).

What is the lie this verse is talking about? The lie, it seems, is a deception regarding the identity of the lawless one, and the message he brings—to free one's self from serving God by becoming a god. And what is the greatest mystery of the UFO phenomenon? The mystery is... the identity of the UFO pilots and what they really want?

When we look at the evidence of UFO and alien encounters there are few creatures that stand up to the physical, spiritual, and dimensional requirements needed to make sense of these beings. Jacques Vallee, one of the premier UFO researchers

has dismissed the theory that these beings are physical extraterrestrials from other planets. Vallee tells us,

"What we see here is not an alien invasion. It is a spiritual system that acts on humans and uses humans."[b]

James A. Walden, an abductee quoted in multiple publications, tells us in his book, *The Ultimate Alien Agenda*,

"Apparently, aliens can transcend time, transform matter, and manipulate human thought and behavior. They can also create distracting illusions to satisfy the needs of our simple human minds." [1]

Whatever is behind the UFO phenomenon, the intelligence that drives them clearly has a handle on the laws of space-time, can transform matter and manipulate human ideology. As we will see in the coming chapters, fallen angels match these traits in every aspect. These beings are extremely powerful, cunning, multi-dimensional, and spiritually driven. Some believe UFOs are a demonic deception. I believe they are angels of the good and fallen variety. Perhaps the angels of old are the UFO pilots of today? Or maybe they are something altogether different. Either way, the angels in scripture, both in service to God and in rebellion, seem to be the primary suspects.

After a thorough investigation, I'm convinced the Bible and other ancient texts connect UFOs and aliens with angels, Satan, and the legions of fallen angels who were banished from heaven. The Bible calls Satan the "ruler of the kingdom of the air" (Ephesians 2:2). He is a ruler because he is not alone; he is accompanied by thousands of similarly powerful angels serving within his kingdom (Revelation 12:3-4), and that makes for the ultimate army of supernatural beings.

As we progress through this book, I hope to show the reader that not only is the Bible connected to these alien beings, but that Jesus, too, has a place in what I call our UFO universe. Although scripture is filled with stories that, to the unbeliever, seem impossible or irrelevant today, I hope to show that the UFO phenomenon is nothing new to the Bible. These craft and the intelligent beings that manipulate our reality were present and active long ago, and they have been warring for our souls from the beginning of our existence in an all-out spiritual battle spearheaded by deception, genetic manipulation, and a desire to supplant God.

In Roger J. Morneau's tell-all account of his experience with a well-to-do satanic organization in Canada, he confirms that one of the primary objectives of the "master" (Lucifer) is to convince humans that fallen angels do not exist. A member of this organization told him,

"We worship spirits, we worship Lucifer and all his angels, and they're just as beautiful as before they were cast out of heaven." ~ Roger J. Morneau

One of the lessons Roger was taught by the high priest around 1945 regarding a coming deception thrusts us directly into our UFO universe, and gives us a glimpse into modern day abduction accounts.

"It's going to be done in an unique manner," the priest said. "This grand plan, people are going to eat this stuff! The spirits will declare themselves to be the inhabitants of far distant planets of the galaxies. They will claim that they have come to warn the inhabitants of planet earth of the impending destruction of earth, unless certain things are done to avoid it." [2]

Roger went on to explain that these people would have out of body experiences and that they'd firmly believe they were taken to distant places, leaving "deep impressions" on their psyches. The high priest told Roger this would be accomplished through the master and his angels' ability to create "highly vivid scenes" in their minds. The outcome of this plan can be seen in Robert Monroe's UFO encounter when he describes an out of body experience:

"I was completely powerless, with no will of my own, and I felt as if I were in the presence of a very strong force, in personal contact with it... It had an intelligence of a form beyond my comprehension... I received the firm impression that I was inextricably bound by loyalty to this intelligent force, always had been, and that I had a job to perform here on earth." Days later when the entities returned, Monroe states, "They seemed to soar up into the sky, while I called after them pleading. Then I was sure that their mentality and intelligence was far beyond my understanding. It is an impersonal, cold intelligence, with none of the love and compassion which we respect so much, yet this may be the omnipotence we call God."[3]

This type of experience is common among abductees' reports and runs parallel with the "impending destruction" mentioned in Morneau's account by the satanic priest, and those that Dr. Karla Turner's retells in her book *Masquerade of Angels*, the true story about Ted Rice's remarkable alien encounters. Claims of forthcoming apocalyptic catastrophes are extremely common, among other explanations. Many abductees are told the aliens need our help, or that they have been manipulating our DNA for the good of the universe, or that they are assisting our evolution to a higher spiritual plane, or that they are helping us to learn how to better manage our planet. Yet at the same time, many abductees experience or witness sexual assault, intrusive medical procedures, and of course all abductions are involuntary acts of kidnapping.

So what do they really want? Our planet? Our DNA? Or our souls?

The message seems to be more contradictory in scope than sincere in principle. If they are attempting to raise our consciousness to a higher level, is kidnapping, rape, and soul snatching the higher consciousness they're referring to? Is that the higher moral experience we are to strive for? And what does our genetic material have to do with saving the planet? In my opinion, this is all too bizarre, too contradictory to be sincere, and just as manipulative in nature as the stories mentioned previously. Somehow, in the midst of these abductions, many are told and believe that what is happening to them is essentially a good thing, despite the evidence to the contrary. The entire experience is absurd as some researchers point out, and yet psychiatrist John E. Mack M.D. (1925-

2004) Pulitzer Prize winning author, agrees that abductees are experiencing a real and impacting phenomenon.

Vallee reports that he knew a stable man that left his life in Los Angeles in obedience to extraterrestrial orders to live in solitude until the "intense turmoil that was to come" subsided.[4] This, too, aligns with what Vallee calls a new form of religion—a "new spiritual movement" based on alien control systems that he believes is immerging among those who affirm we are being visited by benevolent aliens.

The great deception, it seems, is working. A June 28, 2012 FOX News report claims that 1/3 of Americans believe UFOs are real, and that 1/3 believe that aliens have visited earth. That means if you are a skeptic, you are only 2 people away from a believer. Look around—1 out of 12 of your friends and neighbors claim to have seen a UFO, a craft that they believe is not from this planet.[5]

When we revisit Matthew 4, we learn that Satan is capable of teleportation, and creating life-like visions. Clearly unbound to terrestrial soil, fallen angels can sweep their victims up in a whirlwind, taking them from the vast kingdoms of the world to the highest point of the Israeli temple for the exclusive purpose of drawing the soul away from God. If Jesus interacted with a being of this nature, is it really that difficult to believe that others are having the same experiences. Satan, whatever he is—fallen angel, alien, or dimensional enemy of a heavenly state—is still deceiving mankind in the same fashion in which he approached Jesus? Others have undergone a similar deception over time with a different plot connected by similar characters that largely coincide with modern modes of thinking, but still interested in stealing souls.

Both passages reveal the immense power undergirding fallen angels, and they align perfectly with the angelic encounters found in scripture. The same angels that announced the Christ child's birth, also protected Israel from supernatural forces, killed thousands in battle, and soared through the skies like *balls of light*, bright *horses*, and *chariots of fire*. They are God's warriors—the *host of heaven*. They are structured like a powerful military operation with leaders, scouts, messengers, protectors, and worshipers. This is also true among the fallen angels, as they maintain their orders and ranks.

Both sets of angels are equally powerful. Both are equally determined. Both represent supernatural beings that dwell outside our reality. They can enter our physical space, and are just as active today as ever. Could it be the heavenly realms of scripture represent all that is happening in the abduction cases and UFO encounters? I think it certainly is a possibility. And I think we've missed the connection because of the spiritual deception mentioned in scripture. But who can blame us; scripture is often vague about the bizarre nature of our universe even though it mentions some of the greatest conundrums of our time. Hopefully, this examination will shed some light on these mysteries, not to solve them, but to make better sense of what the Bible has to say about them.

~†~

There is a final aspect to Genesis 3:15 that we don't hear much about—the seed. The woman's seed, according to most Christian doctrines, represents the human lineage that would eventually culminate in the birth of Jesus Christ. We follow the ensuing generations in The Old Testament until Jesus' ministry is finally launched four thousand years later. Three years after the temptation in the desert, Genesis 3:15 is finally fulfilled.

Or was it?

Whatever became of the serpent's seed? Is it crushed as promised in the above passage? Yes and no. If the verse was to be interpreted literally, it can be said that Satan "struck Jesus' heel" when the nails were pounded through his feet into the cross. In that case, it can also be said that Jesus struck Satan's head when he defeated sin and death through his crucifixion and resurrection. But if the verse was to be interpreted metaphorically, this is not the end of the story. According to scripture the battle for human souls will not end until Christ returns, finally casting Satan and the fallen angels into the pit of hell, wherever that is.

Is Satan's seed still at enmity against the woman's seed? With so many sexual and genetic experiments reported by alien abductees, it would appear so. UFO and alien investigators report that both male and females are used for genetic manipulation, cloning, and for improving DNA. But who knows what they really want. Although there are general themes that connect abductees' accounts, there are far too many conflicting statements by the alien abductees detailing the claims the aliens have made. It seems as if it's impossible to get an accurate and truthful understanding of their ultimate program.

In her book *Taken: Inside the Alien-Human Agenda*, Dr. Turner documents one abductees' experience with the alien "seed" phenomenon:

"She [Pat] went up to the blond man who was surrounded by a beautiful light. He talked to her about becoming a mother and about a 'seed of life.' He said he had the power of all seed in his hand. At the end of the experience, he held out his hand to her and showed her a seed, telling her it was for her benefit and to have no fear." A few months later, Pat was pregnant.

Pregnancy is obviously not evidence of an alien encounter, but I find it interesting that in this account the alien presents a "seed" that appears significant if not the ultimate purpose for the abduction. Although this may be a trivial coincidence, with little to no bearing on a biblical connection to aliens, it may be one of many telling proofs that the Bible has given us more information about our UFO universe than we've realized.

~†~

Fallen angels, demons, aliens, call them what you will, like a pendulum that swings from one spectrum to another, I believe the battle for our souls will end precisely where it began—in the heavenly realms. And where is that? According to scripture the heavenly realm is the sky above, and the dimensions we cannot see nor understand. The Messianic return, or the coming apocalypse described in the Bible, is without a doubt going to take place in the heavens for all to see; scripture is very clear about that. Even the aliens warn us of this. And should they be concerned? Is it any wonder they warn the abducted ones of future catastrophes? If they are the fallen ones doomed to judgment, they have much to fear!

A coming apocalypse is nothing new to us. Our movies and video games are flooded with apocalyptic zombie themes and projections of the coming end of days. In fact, this is evident not only in western cultures, but across the globe. St. John's Revelation, the Old Testament prophecies, statements made by Jesus himself, and the apocalyptic words of God's good friend, Enoch, foretells Christ's glorious return followed by the final judgment when all mankind and the fallen angels will reap what they have sown. And yet the return of the Messiah is also anticipated by Esoteric Christian teachings, the Church of Jesus Christ of Latter-Day Saints, Jehovah's Witnesses, Ahmadis, Baha'i Faith, Hindu religions, and ancient Aztec cultures. They all anticipate a second coming of the Christ, a Son of God.

The connection between our UFO universe and the second coming may have less to do with similarities among belief systems, and more to do with the unmistakable parallels between the supernatural world we find in the Bible and today's UFO and alien encounters. I'm not the first to observe the similarities. Some call the connection a "demon deception". Jacques Vallee calls it a "control system" meant to manage our spiritual beliefs. And this is precisely what we see in scripture—one system pursues righteousness, and the other is bent on rebellion. Both systems pursue the human soul.

Long before the typical grey alien was first sketched, the famed occultist Aleister Crowley (1875-1947) had drawn an image that very closely represents what we commonly referred to as a grey alien. He called this spiritual entity LAM, and called upon it for wisdom and guidance. Crowley claimed it could materialize out of thin air and acted as a sort of spirit guide. Speaking of this being, Crowley once said, "Today, they call them angels and demons. Tomorrow they'll call them something else."

When reading abductee and contactee reports, the "spirit guide" theme often pops up, along with other supernatural parallels. Many abductees report on-going paranormal activity and/or an increase in extra sensory perception. Is this a coincidence, or another connection between fallen angels and aliens?

John Dee (1527-1609), mathematician, astrologist, and advisor to Queen Elizabeth I, spent many years invoking and communicating with what he originally called "angels". Over time he grew increasingly convinced that these beings were not what they claimed and that he believed they were "lying" to him. As we will see, deception is still common among those who encounter alien beings today.[6]

~†~

This book asks the questions: Are we interacting with the same spirit world described in the Bible under a different disguise? Are we misinterpreting the angels of the Bible as extraterrestrials, or is it the other way around? How will Bible-believing Christians interpret our UFO universe? Are angels and demons part of a multi-verse not yet understood by man? Are the powers and spiritual entities in scripture exactly what they claim to be—spiritual beings in service to a divine creator? Or were angels a foreshadowing of today's extraterrestrials?

I hope to answer these questions in the context that angels, both good and fallen, are the embodiment of the UFO phenomenon. The Bible tells us that Jesus rules over these celestial beings, making him the Admiral of tens of thousands of angelic creatures. Yet as we imagine the glorious beings and their brilliant appearance, we cannot forget the immortal fallen ones doomed for destruction, an equal and opposite force capable of traversing time and space, performing miraculous healings, telepathy, multidimensional travel, altering their appearance, creating/displaying visions, and far more.

Alien encounters today are strikingly similar to angelic and supernatural encounters found in scripture, and throughout recorded history. Both center around a spiritual objective that either draws one near or pulls one away from God. And this is why it is important to me to evaluate where Jesus Christ fits in this spiritual puzzle. To some, Jesus is simply a messenger from another planet, one of many prophets, or a representation of God's repeated manifestations on this earth. Whether you believe that Jesus Christ is the Son of God or not, I believe he is connected to what many people assume is an extraterrestrial invasion of sorts.

~†~

Amidst the thousands of UFO encounters, angels are often overlooked as possible suspects because of common misperceptions. When we think of angels we imagine beautiful creatures that serve as our guardians or chubby babies with wings. They don't seem to fit the extraterrestrial narration, do they? However, when we study biblical angels as a unique entity we learn that good and fallen angels come from the same stuff. And when the fog is lifted, we can see exactly where Jesus and his angels fit in our UFO universe, a place teaming with spiritual entities that have been interacting with men and women through every culture, time period, and religion—entities fighting for our souls—some to keep it— some to steal it.

The stakes are high in this spiritual conflict. Both sides are warring for the part of us that is most difficult to define— a perfect storm—a struggle that many refuse to believe exists—one that is nearly impossible to accept without faith. And yet we are promised a battle of apocalyptic proportions that will bring this war to an end. One side claims that God's work is complete—that the gift of salvation is attained by simply believing in the Son of God. The other side has changed its story over time, matching its appearances and agenda to each culture with a chameleon-like allure that is drawing believers with a different kind of faith.

Simply put, according to scripture Jesus is coming again in a big way to settle the score with these dark spiritual entities. Could these fallen angels be disguised as something else? Are Christians waiting to see Jesus actually floating down on a cloud upon his return? Or will he come back in something a bit more complex? No matter what we imagine about Jesus' return, the Bible consistently testifies about this amazing moment that every man, woman, and child will witness. The prophecy was given to Daniel, Isaiah, Jesus, and Enoch, each referring to the Messiah. Although the prophecy was penned by numerous authors over thousands of years, the message remains the same.

"See the Lord is coming with fire, and his chariots are like a whirlwind; he will bring down his anger with fury, and his rebuke with flames of fire. For with fire and with his sword the Lord will execute judgment upon all men, and many will be slain by the Lord." (Isaiah 66:15-16)

"I looked, and there before me was one like a son of man, coming with the clouds of heaven." (Daniel 7:13)

"And you will see the Son of Man sitting at the right hand of the Mighty One and coming on the clouds of heaven." (*Jesus* - Mark 14:62)

"And behold! He cometh with ten thousands of His holy ones To execute judgment upon all" (Enoch 1:3:9)

"From them I heard all things, and understood what I saw; that which will not take place in this generation, but in a generation which is to succeed at a distant period, on account of the elect. Upon their account I spoke and conversed with him, who will go forth from his habitation, the Holy and Mighty One, the God of the world; Who will hereafter tread upon Mount Sinai; appear with his hosts; and be manifested in the strength of his power from heaven." (Enoch 1:2-6)

"I saw heaven standing open and there before me was a white horse, whose rider is called Faithful and True. With justice he judges and wages war. His eyes are like blazing fire, and on his head are many crowns. He has a name written on him that no one knows but he himself. He is

dressed in a robe dipped in blood, and his name is the Word of God. The armies of heaven were following him, riding on white horses and dressed in fine linen, white and clean. Coming out of his mouth is a sharp sword with which to strike down the nations." (Revelation 19:11-15)

The next passage may surprise you. According to Hindu texts, the final manifestation of God on earth will come in the appearance of Lord Kalki, the 10th and final avatar, who will come to judge mankind for the evil done upon the earth. Is it a coincidence that this passage is written in a similar manner and in the same context as the Judeo-Christian prophecy?

"Lord Kalki, the Lord of the universe, will mount His swift white horse Devadatta and, sword in hand, travel over the earth exhibiting His eight mystic opulences and eight special qualities of Godhead. Displaying His unequaled effulgence and riding with great speed, He will kill by the millions those thieves who have dared dress as kings."[7]

Did you notice the key words throughout the above texts?

Armies of Heaven.

Rider on a white horse.

White horses.

Flaming fire.

Coming on the clouds.

Whirlwinds.

All of these terms are indicative of God's Holy Army—His angels. These terms, among others, are used frequently in scripture whenever angels are present, and tell us what to expect when Christ returns. Besides presenting evidence that the angels in the Bible fit the modern day UFO descriptions, I hope to demonstrate that the Bible passages ancient astronaut theorists use to claim that UFOs were present in antiquity, are actually describing angels both fallen and in service to God. The evidence will be presented in waves, slowly building up to a crescendo with one concept setting the stage for the next surge of information.

Because the subject matter is so controversial and the premise so outlandish, I believe it is important to serve my theory in segments. First, I will discuss the reality of the UFO phenomenon because without a clear understanding of what is being reported there is no system to compare the biblical account to. Next, I will begin contrasting UFO and abduction accounts with biblical and logical arguments, so as to set up the angelic connection. And finally, after detailing the angels described in scripture and their place in the UFO universe, I will demonstrate that Jesus, the Prince of angels, is the main protagonist in this story, a supernatural sci-fi adventure that spans both time and space.

2.

OFFICIAL ACCOUNTS

Contrast biblical prophecies with today's world of ufology and you'll get a strikingly different picture. Ufologists are not awaiting the second coming of Christ; they're waiting for the United States government to disclose all of its documentation about UFOs and aliens. They're waiting for the US government to admit that UFOs are real, that they have alien craft and bodies in their possession, and that they have access to the technologies behind these craft.

There certainly are plenty of witnesses who can attest to this. So what does this mean in light of our human existence? Are we alone in this ever-expanding universe? Are we one among many races? I don't have the answer to that question. I do know that real people attest to personal alien encounters, and many claim to have personally witnessed UFOs that cannot be explained away by weather balloons, satellites, or swamp gas. I also know that familiar characters in the Bible had similar encounters.

~†~

Can you imagine if the entire world were told in an official manner that aliens are living among us—that extraterrestrials from other planets are actually visiting earth? Think of the changes that could occur in our communities, scientific laws, and religions, if alien races began open dialogue with our world leaders, informing us that this universe is populated beyond our imagination, and that God is non-existent. We'd re-write history books and gain a whole new understanding of the cosmos. Some would call it a fresh start, and fully embrace our visitors. Everything would change.

Or would it?

Oh, we'd still work at our day jobs and live our lives, if you look on the positive side, but for the most part we'd do what we do with an entirely different purpose, under a completely different paradigm depending on what the aliens tell us. And here lies one of the more important questions— can we trust them, who or whatever they are?

If this scenario did occur, there could be those who'd hope, or assume I suppose, that mankind would experience a second awakening, an exciting renaissance, and a world filled with wonder. Global interest in space programs would shoot to the moon. Math, science, and astrophysics majors would become rock stars. Sexy extraterrestrials would quickly become celebrities. NASA employees with an inside track could ask ungodly speaking fees from those interested in knowing how it all came about, and what to expect from our visitors.

On the other hand, what about those who hold a firm belief that aliens are not what they claim to be? What will become of those who believe that God created the earth, and that we are not the handiwork of an alien race? How would the world respond? How would the aliens treat the nonconformists? Would they understand and appreciate our numerous long-held beliefs about faith and our origins regardless of their presence? Or, would the faithful be exterminated?

The battles and resistance to follow would be like nothing this earth has ever seen. We humans are far too independent and determined to bow down to cosmic creatures. Blood, both human and alien, would fill the streets of every nation.

That would be truly frightening. But that's just fiction— isn't it? Of course it is. That's how I imagine it, anyway. Still, something is going on.

UFO sightings are increasing rapidly. They are real, and stories of alien abductions are silently on the rise. So what's occurring? If aliens exist, where does Jesus Christ fit in, if at all? With thousands of UFO sightings, and alleged alien visitations popping up every year, the world is beginning to wonder what is real, and if we are alone. The world wants answers because if we are not alone in the universe, it could mean that everything we've known is false. If we have space brothers and sisters, and if extraterrestrials exist on other planets or in other dimensions, people may want to reconsider their belief systems. If this is the case, we will be forced to ask if Jesus is who he said he was, or if his existence was completely misinterpreted? Was Jesus an alien sent here by a caring space family with supernatural abilities, or was he the God that he claimed to be? And if he is God, where does he fit in among the extraterrestrials that seem to be presently visiting our planet? If extraterrestrials exist, Jesus is less likely to be God, and his historical and spiritual significance could eventually fade over time. But if these beings are angels, then Jesus stands out as the most significant player in our UFO universe because according to scripture, he commands the angels and they bow at the sound of his name.

If you want to understand how Jesus fits into a UFO universe, you'll have to look at Scripture in a "new context". What I mean is, if we study the Bible with the understanding that extra-dimensional beings, whatever they are, exist and inter-dimensional travel is possible, many of the biblical tales spring to life. On the flip side, many of the illustrations in scripture may appear silly or mythical to those who do not believe there's something going on up there in our big blue sky because there are plenty of passages that go unanswered if the phenomenon is dismissed.

I believe the passages in scripture that delve into the strange and curious world of angels and "Watchers" are too often overlooked or ignored because of the absurdity they present. Do angels appear as balls of fire? Can they shine like burning metal in the same way many people have described UFOs? Do they zig and zag across the sky and zip away straight up into the heavens? If so, is there evidence of this in the Bible?

Yes.

Let's examine what's happening today. This will give us a point of reference to compare biblical accounts against modern reports.

~†~

To discover what's happening, we must start somewhere even if we can't all agree on what's behind the UFO phenomenon. If you ignore the UFO universe that's being reported and recorded more and more each year, you will miss a key reality to God's power and supernatural existence. It's imperative that Christians fully understand what's going on because the UFO reality is a very powerful phenomenon. It's strange, supernatural, and physical, whether you like it (or believe it) or not.

Solomon said that there's nothing new under the sun, and that is just as true today as it was in 950 BC. Today we know that there were thriving civilizations all around the world when Moses and the prophets roamed the Promised Land. This is very important to consider because some of these cultures mention some strange beings and depict what some interpret as spacecraft in their art and literature. Scripture, too, mentions what many interpret as UFOs and alien beings. It's as if the author assumed the reader had knowledge about what was going on in the heavens. And there is valuable information hidden in the original Hebrew text that casual students of the Bible miss; like the meanings behind names of clans, or assumptions about the starry hosts. This can be frustrating because if a casual reader comes across an anomaly in scripture like a flying chariot, we are left to modern commentary, and biblical scholars rarely delve into the strange occurrences found in scripture. Therefore, I believe studying the Bible with a UFO context actually gives the text more credibility, and could be more appealing to open-minded seekers in a post-disclosure economy.

Accepting the new context (i.e. the acceptance of UFOs guided by intelligent beings) is a step to not only growing one's faith, but in equipping one's self with the tools to respond to the questions that are sure to arise upon disclosure, or more importantly in conversations with others hooked on ancient alien theories.

High-Profile Witnesses

If the latest UFO and alien research is new to you, you've had to work very hard to avoid it. The global distribution of information coming from cable networks, YouTube, and the Internet have made the data extremely easy to acquire. This has certainly attributed to the explosion of information, research, and evidence. But make no mistake about it; the web has also paved the way for false reports, blatant mockery, and disinformation.

Regardless of the outright denials and contradictory reports out there, it is imperative we look at the same evidence governments and institutions are utilizing. It seems to me that disclosing a false UFO universe would be the last thing responsible governments would do. In fact, disclosure has traditionally been a point of contention because governments feared that citizens would respond in a negative manner. As global citizens begin to accept the possibility that we are not alone, thanks to science (Hubble/research), the governments listed below believe that the world is now capable of handling the truth. The US, however, does not.

To help you understand how real, the debate is, I'd like to list a few quotations from military and intelligence officials who have stepped forward to expose our UFO universe.

Gordon Cooper, a Gemini and Mercury astronaut was quoted in the July 28, 2009 edition of the examiner.com. "*A saucer flew right over, put down three landing gears, and* landed on the dry lakebed. [The cameramen] went out there with their cameras towards the UFO. It lifted off and flew off at a very high rate of speed... I had a chance to hold [the film] up to the window. Good close-up shots. There was no doubt that it was made someplace other than on this earth."[8]

Edgar Mitchell, an Apollo 14 astronaut, admitted in a July 2008 ABC News interview, *"The UFO phenomenon is real,"* and, *"It has been covered up by governments for quite some time now."* Mitchell further stated, *"I have been privileged enough to be in on the fact that we have been visited on this planet."*

Mitchell has also appeared on Larry King Live, one of the few major media programs that give high-profile witnesses a platform to speak about this topic. Most media outlets simply ignore statements like this... But isn't that newsworthy?

High profile admission isn't anything new. On February 28, 1960, former **CIA Director, Admiral R.H. Hillenkoetter** told the New York Times, "It is time for the truth to be brought out in open Congressional hearings. Behind the scenes, high-ranking Air Force officers are soberly concerned about UFOs. But through official secrecy and ridicule, citizens are led to believe the unknown flying objects are nonsense. To hide the facts, the Air Force has silenced its personnel." And they are still doing so today.

Dr. Richard Haines, NASA Research Scientist (Gemini, Apollo, Skylab): "Air Catalogue is a rather extensive library I've been collecting for almost thirty years from commercial, private, and test pilots. I have over three thousand cases. My estimate is that for every pilot who does come forward, and makes a confidential or public report [regarding UFOs], there are twenty, thirty other pilots who won't."[9]

In an interview during the filming of the Sirius documentary, **Don Philips,** private pilot and formerly USAF, CIA, and engineer with Lockheed Skunkworks, spoke about an experience early on in his career near Area 51, circa 1961. "I looked up in the air and saw these objects... lighted objects, moving at tremendous speeds... it's like what we would know as special effects today. And it was in the area slightly to the north and northwest of Mt. Charleston... All of a sudden I said, 'wow what an aerial show'... But right at the instant when I saw these things making acute angles and traveling, eh maybe I would estimate, three to four thousand miles per hour, and then immediately making a acute turn, I knew they weren't ours. And I had the special background with the Skunkworks, Lockheed Aircraft advanced development and engineering that said, 'These are not ours.' And having been a pilot I'm thinking what kind of forces these uh, if they were people in these craft, what kind of forces their bodies are taking. And I said, 'Well these have to be guided by some type of, intelligent pilot, if you will... And then all of a sudden, they seemed to group from what would be hundreds of miles in the sky to the east or to the west and they came into a circle, rotated in a circle and disappeared... As far as the inhabitants thereof we don't know."

U.S. Presidents have also mentioned or personally witnessed UFOs. **President Harry Truman**: "Oh yes we discussed it at every conference that we had with the military... and they never were able to make me a concrete report on the subject... There's always things like that going on, eh flying saucers and we've had other things you know, if I'm not mistaken."[10] In 1950 President Truman also said, "I can assure you that flying saucers, given that they exist, are not constructed by any power on earth." [11]

There is a chance that governments could have high tech craft that the average citizen (or soldier) is not aware of, but it is not very likely that we have the technology to manufacture craft that appear as balls of fire, star-like spheres, or any vessel that can vanish in the blink of an eye. This points out an interesting issue: With so many sightings we would expect to see heavy traffic in our solar system. However, this is not the case. In fact, the absence of "traffic", among other considerations, is leading more researchers to believe that UFOs are not guided by flesh and blood extraterrestrials, but rather by some kind of ultra-dimensional being. It is this, and other evidence, that leads me back to angels.

Harry Truman is not alone. Other presidents have been quoted on the subject of UFOs. In 1973, referring to a UFO sighting witnessed alongside several others, **Jimmy Carter** said, "There were about twenty of us standing outside of a little restaurant, I believe, a high school lunch room, and a kind of green light appeared in the western sky. This was right after sundown. It got brighter and brighter. And then it eventually disappeared. It didn't have any solid substance to it; it was just a very peculiar-looking light. None of us could understand what it was."

Recalling an event in 1974 while flying in a Cessna piloted by Bill Paynter on route to Bakersfield, CA, **Ronald Reagan** (still Governor of California) said to Norman C. Miller (Washington bureau for the Wall Street Journal, "We followed it for several minutes. It was a bright white light. We followed it to Bakersfield, and all of a sudden to our utter amazement it went straight up into the heavens."[12]

UFO and alien encounters have been occurring for hundreds of years. One of the best books I've read documenting historical UFO accounts is *Dimensions* by Jacques Vallee. The author dates some of the earliest written accounts long before 1947. In a period spanning 600 years, there were many reports in Japan detailing UFO sightings. In 989 AD three "round objects of unusual brilliance" were seen in the sky and later converged into one object. In 1458 five multi-colored "stars" were viewed "circling the moon". Witnesses claimed the stars changed colors as many as three times and later disappeared.[13] Vallee includes encounters in Texas in 1878, in Germany in 1577, and an abduction report in Spain, 779, by one of the most "learned and prelates of the ninth century" who claimed that 4 humans were abducted and returned days later. The author also documents a 1768 account by 3 travelers going to the University of Leipzig who saw several lights "gleaming" that "jumped about here and there, as well downwards from above as vice versa, and in every direction."

The above records were documented long before the first flight in 1903. The earliest UFO sighting I found recorded in history books was in 214 BC by the Roman historian Livy, who documented the "phantom ships gleaming in the sky" in book 21 of The History of Rome, or the Urbe Condita Libri.[14] Other reports as early as 74 and 70 BC include a sighting in Jerusalem recorded in the War of the Jews by historian Josephus in which "there appeared in the air over the whole country chariots and armed troops coursing through the clouds, surrounding the cities." [15]

Vallee documents many more reports including "alien" and "spacecraft" type sightings that date as far back as 30 AD by one of the Christian Church fathers. Some of the craft sighted in the Middle Ages were described as flying earthenware, balls of light, stars, flying hats, egg-shaped and saucer-shaped craft with landing gear ranging from wagon wheels to tripods. These craft were generally reported to have been piloted by small alien beings (3' to 5') equipped with everything from beards and hooves, to the clichéd dark, emotionless eyes, and immobilizing light wands. In most cases the craft and pilots witnessed in UFO landing reports seemed to change to suit the time and culture. The messages received by the contactees were much the same—evolving to match the culture. Of course there are thousands of reports at sites like MUFON.com and thousands more reported each year, with nearly 3% of Americans reporting that they have been abducted by some form of alien race, usually the Grey,

Reptilian, Nordic, or tall Whites. There are so many UFO reports and claims of abduction that it could make your head spin!

I have pointed out modern and historical accounts not because I'm trying to prove the existence of UFO and alien encounters. I will leave that investigative journey to the reader under the assumption that he or she is already somewhat of a believer, or at least interested in the subject. The point is that this is a real phenomenon, and is under severe scrutiny at the highest levels of government. I am also showing, although too briefly for my own comfort, that UFO and extraterrestrial encounters are not new. In fact, many researchers will point out artifacts and encounters that go much further back in time than I have presented.

Taking it all in

If you are a Christian I assume you trust eyewitness accounts, because the Christian faith rests upon eyewitness testimony. So taking the quotations above into consideration, we must ask the question: How does Jesus fit into a universe teeming with life, when people of such high caliber tell us that UFOs are real, and there are possibly extraterrestrials visiting this planet? What are these things—UFOs and aliens? Are they from other planets, another dimension, or something else altogether?

Why ask the questions to begin with? Why not leave well enough alone? Because I've been interested in ufology for some time, and the more I learn, the more I've been forced to ask the questions that all religions will grapple with if the existence of intelligent beings is announced.

The reason I think it is so important to start talking about this is because I believe disclosure of alien existence (however they are defined) is imminent, whether by design or by an unmistakable event. And if you have ignored the topic of UFO's and extraterrestrial life, you may not know that many countries have fully disclosed their documentation regarding UFO and extraterrestrial encounters. To date, over 20 countries have officially announced that UFO's are on their investigative radars. The countries that have chosen to reveal what they know may surprise you.[16]

1. Argentina
2. Australia
3. Brazil
4. Canada
5. Chile
6. China
7. Denmark
8. Finland
9. France
10. Germany
11. India
12. Ireland
13. Japan
14. Mexico
15. New Zealand
16. Peru
17. Russia
18. Spain

19. Sweden

20. Ukraine

21. United Kingdom

22. Uruguay

23. Vatican City

If you've never heard that these countries (including the UN) desire open disclosure, it is not evidence that the phenomenon does not exist. Understandably, the topic gets buried, and buried fast. You truly need to study fringe news and literature to get this information. In essence, I'm simply pointing out the fact that UFO disclosure could be on the horizon, and is looming over your church or personal convictions. And by the time this book is published, there will be many more sightings. Furthermore, it's possible that if these "beings" make themselves known to all mankind, or if they cooperate with governments in a global "reveal" or "unmasking", a cataclysmic change in religious philosophies will occur or be forced by rule of law. And this could happen, even among the "saints", because most people will not be able to logically dismiss the deceit. And I believe that this system is a very real and complex deception.

As stated in 2 Thessalonians 2:9, *"The coming of the lawless one will be in accordance with how Satan works. He will use all sorts of displays of power through signs and wonders that serve the lie..."*

Although I believe the phenomenon is partly a deception, I also believe that many UFO sightings could be the natural appearance of all types of angels—good and fallen, because they are made from the same cloth. In either case, UFO visitations are very much real to those who have the courage to speak out about their experiences. One only needs to read the daily updates at MUFON.com among many UFO watchdog/reporting sites to grasp the magnitude of the sightings.

Normal, sane people of all types are reporting and videoing their experiences every day, including those in official positions. Many reports can be explained, but many cannot. Quality reports have numerous levels of evidence such as multiple eyewitnesses that coincide with official air traffic control, television news footage, and identical reports that follow the trajectory of flight sometimes covering several cities, states, or military bases. Of course, many sightings can be dismissed for a variety of reasons, but there are too many to ignore at this point. You may not have seen a UFO, and dismiss alien visitations altogether, but a strange reality has millions of eyes across the world fixated on the heavens. Some report their encounters to the authorities; some do not, fearing public ridicule. Yet scholars believe that these people are rational, honest, sane people who've encountered something real and unexplainable.

I'm convinced that whatever results disclosure may bring, everyone will have to reckon with UFOs and the creatures behind the star-like objects we see overhead. If mankind comes to terms with the fact that we share our reality with intelligent, non-human beings, we will all have to contemplate our origins, purpose, and spirituality. And this, I believe, could be the ultimate purpose behind the phenomenon—to change our perceptions about God—to draw us away from our Creator.

Why would God allow this to continue? Why would he allow the abuctees to suffer as they have? In my opinion, God is allowing the "lie" to persist, in his ultimate sovereignty, so that mankind will look to the heavens, seek answers, and find HIM in the process?

3.

FACTS & FAULTS

To fully understand why ufology is significant to me, and ultimately to you, we need to study the phenomenon itself and the many ideas and theories surrounding these strange occurrences. Only then can you discern the picture that emerges when all the parts come together. As I have learned, restricting one's input to the History, Sci-fi, or Discovery Channels is not a good idea. The thing is, you can't simply go back to the Roswell case and move forward from there. This is much more complex. Human interaction with these beings goes back to the beginning of recorded history, so it's important that we not only examine modern interaction, and abduction cases, but historical texts as well.

Before the Admiral takes his proper place in the Heavens, we need to wade through the facts, deep and murky as they may be. But I'll warn you; the ocean of ideas on this subject can smash you like a tsunami. Once the waves of information hit, they keep coming, faster and deeper until you're drowning in details and suppositions that can ultimately leave you more confused than when you started. So let's start with a few basic ideas about the phenomenon.

~†~

The Christian faith is very egocentric in terms of the believer's view of God as a loving Father who is deeply concerned with the individual, so the belief that we are random, a lowly race among millions, or formed out of chaos is unimaginable to the average believer, thereby leaving some Christians with the belief that alien life is not very likely. If this is you, fear not; as we soar with these beings, you may discover that you are far more significant than you realize.

It's no secret that Christianity is built upon a monotheistic view that there is one God, and He created the earth and the entire cosmos for His pleasure and for those He created here on earth—with little mention of extraterrestrial life. Furthermore, it is believed that the Bible is the final word regarding our Genesis, and that God's plan for humanity as written in the Old and New Testament is the Alpha and Omega—the beginning and the end of our story. Because of this teaching, it is quite a stretch for a born-again Christian to believe that there is more to this world outside of eternal glory or damnation, resigning the only realm outside of our terrestrial existence to Heaven, Hell, and the vast "dead space" out there in an empty universe. Conversely, this belief seems primitive and uncompromising to the ufologist and ancient alien theorist. Most ufologists seem hungry to discover life in the cosmos. But could it be that the life they are searching for is found in the Bible, already recorded for thousands of years by highly trained scribes? Could the spiritual entities they hope to discover be the dimensional beings known as angels?

~†~

Judeo-Christian beliefs are going to become more of an obstacle amidst a looming global UFO disclosure, and frankly, hated by the world if Christians or other faiths hold to their beliefs in the face of "disclosure". If we can trust Roger J. Morneau's account about a satanic plot, a new "religious system" would be disastrous for Christians.

As you will see, to deny the UFO phenomenon is to deny the supernatural world within the context of the Bible, and the world in which we live. As this book unfolds, I'll address the questions regarding Christianity's place in a UFO universe, why it's okay that we're not alone, and point out that scripture and other early church documents have given us a glimpse into this reality. For it seems that preachers and prophets have misinterpreted, overlooked, or disregarded our place in the heavens buzzing with spiritual activity. Sadly, Christianity has also disregarded the book of Enoch and other highly read books from the early church that allude to a history where humans interact with dimensional beings and what many consider UFOs. It seems to me that in our effort to demonize religions and cultures that fill historical gaps with UFO imagery such as Hindu Vedas and Aztec rituals, we've missed an important part of our story.

It's quite possible that we are not alone. Our universe is far bigger than we can imagine. Yet if Scripture does not acknowledge UFOs and extraterrestrials or anything of that nature, then God has certainly left us without the proper amount of change to unilaterally buy into His Bible story. However, I don't believe that's the case. We've been given hints, signs, and evidence of a UFO universe from the first chapter of Genesis to the last page of Revelation. Yet in our zeal to discover something new, an exciting frontier, we've overlooked evidence that was already collected long ago.

This is not to say that we are the sole fruit of Creator God. To believe that would be the pinnacle of our arrogance. Conversely, the unwillingness of science to accept the supernatural could be their principle weakness in understanding life's greatest mysteries, and possibly misinterpreting a mystery that the Bible has made plain for thousands of years. So could it be that the truth lies somewhere between science and the supernatural?

No matter what you believe about life, eternity, God, human origins, and our universe, I plead with you to set your preconceived ideas aside until you have taken in all the pieces presented here. It's a big universe, and there are far too many unknowns in our past and in our understanding of the laws of physics for anyone to know all the answers without a shadow of doubt, and certainly without a hint of faith—in religion, science, or otherwise.

How Big is our Universe?

The Associated Press published a report on November 5, 2013 in Foxnews.com that states, "Astronomers using NASA data have calculated for the first time that in our galaxy alone, there are at least 8.8 billion stars with Earth-size planets in habitable temperature zones. For perspective, that's more Earth-like planets than there are people on Earth. As for what it says about the odds that there is life somewhere out there, it means 'just in our Milky Way galaxy alone, that's 8.8 billion throws of the biological dice,'" said Geoff Marcy, from the University of California at Berkeley.[17]

With 200 billion stars in our galaxy, the study made a low-ball estimate (not their term) at over 17% hospitable planets, with a potential of up to over 40 Billion inhabitable planets. If that isn't front-page news, I don't know what is. From a Biblical perspective, that's a lot of fertile soil at the Creator's fingertips, and I can't see God wasting a perfectly good garden. You could look at this news as proof of God's power, which it is, but it is also eye opening, indicating the possibility of universal life.

But is the likelihood of alien existence really cutting edge? The concept of UFOs is not new to countries like India, South America, the Middle East, and other countries where alien/god interaction with humans is deeply embedded in their history and culture dating back thousands of years. Yet for the mainstream US citizen, UFO's have been considered taboo for decades. Sightings have been marginalized, and a topic reserved for folks wearing aluminum foil hats, as demonstrated by Governor Fife Symington's 1997 response to the Arizona lights in a press conference when he outfitted a staff member in an alien suit, mocking over 10,000 Arizonians who witnessed one of the most incredible mass UFO sightings ever recorded on film. The Governor would later recant and fully admit that he did in fact see unidentified flying objects of vast proportions. And it should be obvious to any watcher of mainstream media that UFO sightings are rarely included in the programming even though there are thousands of reports world-wide, and over 7,100 UFO sightings in the United States documented by NUFORC (National UFO Reporting Center) in 2014 at the time of this writing (February 2014). Having said that, there are many more local news agencies reporting UFO sightings. These reports can easily be viewed on YouTube by the hundreds, maybe thousands.

What's really sad is, despite the evidence that has been presented around the globe, the White House has joined the information blockade, demonstrating the high-level secrecy that is strangely apparent in the US, although not so much in other industrial nations. This can be seen in a statement recorded in the April 29, 2013 edition of theguardian.com where the following statement from the White House was published: "There is no evidence that any life exists outside our planet, or that an extraterrestrial presence has contacted or engaged any member of the human race... In addition, there is no credible information to suggest that any evidence is being hidden from the public's eye."

It must be disheartening to those who have had first-hand experiences with UFOs and alien encounters. Imagine if you were one of the 10,000 folks in Arizona, or a pilot in the US Air Force, or a citizen who recorded a UFO with his or her camera. To be told by your government that what you've seen and documented is not "credible" must be terribly discouraging.

Why the longstanding US concealment? Well, that's another issue all together, and there are plenty of theories surrounding how and why. But I'm not going there—not very deep anyway. Once you've researched UFO's long enough to accept them as a real part of our existence, you move on to the bigger questions at hand. A decade—quite possibly millennia—of cover-ups is an important topic that should be discussed, and certainly more so as the public becomes educated in the matter; it's just not the main subject I'm addressing.

When considering the global management of such an enormous revelation, studying the sociological response is also worthy of investigation, and governments and institutions have done their due diligence in the matter. But that's not what this book is about, either. This book was specifically written to ask how UFO disclosure could impact our spiritual beliefs.

There are questions that need to be asked, such as:

- Are the aliens aware of God?

- Is Jesus exclusive to the inhabitants of this earth?

- Does the Bible reference the UFO phenomenon?

Some readers may think it's ridiculous to ask these questions because it's obvious that I cannot provide all the answers in this book. And I'm okay with that; God's grace is sufficient. I will not ever state in this book that I am without a doubt correct in all my assertions. We all want answers, and perhaps our various perspectives can ultimately give us what we're looking for. When discussing the truth about alien existence, including who and what they are, and why they're here, no single group desires to understand these beings more than those who have been abducted by them, for their experiences range from benevolent to malevolent and highly sadistic beings.

There are, however, some very valid points I've seen by some researchers that rule out the possibility of "extraterrestrial" visitations. Many of the arguments are related to the problems with space travel, the effects it has on the physical body, and the fact that most UFOs end up dematerializing rather than simply flying off into the sunset. From what we know about physics (at this point), physical bodies cannot handle the rates of speed that is required for intergalactic space travel. Then of course there are the biological problems extraterrestrials would surely encounter such as deadly earth-born viruses, or a non-viable atmosphere that would threaten their lives. These ideas lead me and other researchers to believe that there is another form of travel possible that we have not yet conceived, or that multi-dimensional travel occurs through wormholes, dimensional portals, or that they, whoever they are, reside in a parallel universe, or multiple parallel universes. Could this be the way heaven works, just outside of our grasp, yet all around us? Or is heaven a tangible place, a planet of sorts—a multidimensional reference point where all of God's spiritual entities take flight?

These points lead me to believe that whatever is "out there" has dimensional capabilities, and that they are not simply journeying across outer space to get here. Jacques Vallee has made it very clear that he believes UFOs and their inhabitants are not only dimensional in nature, but that they are likely a psychological manipulation. He has assembled a massive collection of evidence demonstrating the non-physical aspect of these craft, the absurd nature of the beings associated with them, and that statistical impossibility that they are entering our atmosphere. He's also investigated the "super physics" of UFOs, the exacting historical accounts that mirror the UFO and alien phenomenon, and the "pitfalls" in the abduction accounts. Vallee sums up pages of speculation about these flaws in the following statement:

"Let us forget these problems and take all the material at face value. Do we obtain a picture that suggests extraterrestrial contact with advanced visitors? My answer is an emphatic *no*. I asked earlier: what kind of spacecraft pilots are these, if they still have to use maps to navigate [referring to the Betty and Barney Hill case]? Now I have to ask: what kind of doctors are these, who need to induce such trauma in hundreds of patients to collect a little blood, a few embryos?"[18]

The problems that exist in a thorough study of the phenomenon are what generate such vastly different opinions about the subject, and make it difficult to present valid facts, although Vallee has compiled one of the largest individual collections of UFO and abduction statistics. And with that data he has come to the following conclusions:

"I believe that the UFO phenomenon represents evidence for other dimensions beyond space-time; the UFOs may not come from ordinary space, but from a multiverse which is all around us, and of which we have stubbornly refused to consider the disturbing reality in spite of the evidence available to us for centuries.... I believe there is a system around us that transcends time as it transcends space. Other scholars have reached the same conclusion."[19]

The problem with a "multiverse theory" is that if UFOs can appear in our reality and suddenly disappear, as if it were a random act of nature, we would expect to see the occasional glimpse into *their* world, such as aliens cooking dinner and the like—that is, unless those interacting with us have control over the multiverse. But we do not see that, do we? Our interaction with the phenomenon is entirely too predictable to be a result of chance overlaps of reality. The pattern is fairly predictable: UFOs appear, pilots gather something (human or otherwise), contact is made or averted, UFO takes off at alarming speeds and eventually vanishes. In my opinion, this rules out a random interconnection between dimensions, and demonstrates a deliberate spiritual agenda by agents with authority over space and time. According to Vallee this has continued throughout history. And this control over the inner workings of the universe sounds a lot like the God described in the Bible. The intentional spiritual agenda aligns with scripture as well, and the vehicles involved act much the same way as the angels.

Vallee cites vast amounts of evidence pointing not only to the supernatural and paranormal activity associated with the UFO phenomenon, but also the ability of the craft and beings to change their appearance. And as we will soon discover, sounds a lot like angels, too! However, Vallee directly states, "When I speak of a spiritual control system I do not mean that some higher super-civilization has locked us inside the constraints of a space-bound jail, closely monitored by entities we might call angels or demons."

When I read Vallee's ultimate conclusions, it seems as if he believes everything about the phenomenon looks like the angels and demons in scripture, but he refuses to acknowledge these spiritual creatures as the source. The biblical connections found in his research run incredibly deep, at times mirroring a timeline of human occultism, paralleling fallen angels, demons, and the spiritual battle mapped out in the Bible. Very few researchers venture out of ufology (science) and into the biblical records (supernatural) in spite of the supernatural proclivity of the UFO phenomenon. This is one reason why I was reluctant to publish this book at first. But there's too much overlapping data to ignore. In truth, if you re-name fallen angels, and call them "aliens", you have the same phenomenon, the same story with the same plot, same characters, same conflict, and the same agenda outlined in chapter one of Genesis—no more God.

4.

CHURCH & UFOs

If you think the conversation about aliens is reserved for schmucks, "Trekkies", and tin-foil-hat goons who consider Area 51 their spiritual Mecca, you might want to reconsider that notion. A serious discussion is taking place in Rome because the Vatican is taking a UFO universe to heart. Perhaps they have been informed by the powers that be that it is time to begin preparing their over 1-billion member flock for disclosure, or maybe they've simply taken the UFO phenomenon seriously? Either way, the discussion is ongoing in the Vatican and Rome is listening very closely.

A November 11, 2009 cbsnews.com report quotes Rev. Jose Gabriel Funes, an astronomer and director of the Vatican Observatory as saying, *"The questions of life's origins and of whether life exists elsewhere in the universe are very suitable and deserve serious consideration."* Funes also stated, *"Just as there is a multitude of creatures on Earth, there could be other beings, even intelligent ones, created by God. This does not contradict our faith, because we cannot put limits on God's creative freedom."*

The Catholic Church, the CBS report claims, has been meeting for some time now, discussing the implications of extraterrestrial existence in 2005, and then again in 2009 with 30 astronomers, physicists, biologists and other experts who discussed the origins of life in the cosmos.

In a round table discussion in April 2000 in Bellaria, Italy, at a conference aptly titled, *The Mysteries of Human Existence*, speaker, and author Zecharia Sitchin met with top Vatican theologian, Monsignor Corrado Balducci to discuss the UFO and extraterrestrial existence.

In that discussion, Balducci told Sitchin, "That life may exist on other planets is certainly possible... The Bible does not rule out that possibility. On the basis of scripture and on the basis of our knowledge of God's omnipotence, His wisdom being limitless, we must affirm that life on other planets is possible." According to Sitchin, Balducci also said, "When I talk about Extraterrestrials, we must think of beings who are like us—more probably, beings more advanced than us, in that their nature is an association of a material part and a spiritual part, a body and a soul, although in different proportions than human beings on Earth."[19b]

The two men went on to discuss UFOs and the Anunnaki, but I'm especially interested in Balducci's second quote. It sounds like he has an inside track. His description of an advanced race parallels those described by military personnel who have had UFO encounters, and those who claim to have been abducted. Could it be that Balducci knows more than he is leading on to? I'm asking this because in my opinion, if a biblical scholar examines the UFO phenomenon, I would think he or she would test his findings against scripture because there is a lot of evidence in the Bible that mirrors UFO encounters. And yet Balducci doesn't reference the specific points in scripture that I will show you.

In an interview with Dr. Stephen Greer as part of The Disclosure Project, Balducci stated, "We have come to the point that we can't anymore deny that there is something that is happening, that something is happening here in this field of Ufology, not just flying saucers, but there might be actual people, beings, extraterrestrial beings..."

That's what's coming from the Vatican. If you research deeper into the Catholic stance on UFOs, you'll discover that Catholic Leadership is generally open to the idea of life outside of earth, and that the Church would be willing to baptize an alien.

I'm very troubled by the Catholic Church's stance on this subject because Vallee found much of his historical evidence in Catholic archives and much of that evidence points to the impossibility of interplanetary space travel, reinforcing a multidimensional possibility rather than a simple "extraterrestrial" theory. With that as the case, I'm curious why the Catholic Church would hold hundreds of years of evidence that mirrors the UFO phenomenon—evidence that points to angelic-type beings—and suddenly treating the topic as nothing more than a case of intergalactic mission work? Why are they not pointing the church to scripture? There is a lot of evidence there. Even if there is life on other planets, the Bible presents a very strong case that much of what we see in the sky could be angels—an active partner in the faith. So unless God and angels are dead, a historical figment of our imagination, we should still take a long hard look at what scripture tells us about UFOs.

What does Evangelical Christianity have to say about the UFO Phenomena? This is of particular interest to me because that's where I fit in, and from where my query originates.

For starters, the topic isn't new to Christian thinkers. In a 1950s article in the *Christian Herald, C.S. Lewis* revealed a hint of Exotheism when he wrote that the Son of God could have come from another planet. He assumed the other option is that God simply formulated separate plans of salvation for all life forms, including those that may exist in other life systems.[20] The concept is yet another alternative to consider, if the God of Christianity is the same God behind the creation of extraterrestrials.

Questioning where God and Jesus fit into a universal philosophy (philosophy in the face of universal life) is such an important issue because God as creator of all things is a major doctrine for Christians and must be dealt with particularly in the context of disclosure, not because the existence of extraterrestrials proves or disproves God's existence, but because it matters. The answer matters to me, and I'm sure it matters to anyone else interested in this topic. And yet there is a danger in accepting an alien's perspective, because asking an extraterrestrial about God could be like asking a scorpion if oceans exist. The answers could be vast, biased, or deceptive.

Unfortunately I think there's a perception out there that if aliens exist, God must not. But since we have not been given the universal truth about life outside our planet, we should be careful about attaching disclosure with atheism. After all, the general consensus is that these beings are self-confessed spiritualists. But is that good enough for us to trust them? What if the visitors are religious about survival? You see, the concept that extraterrestrial existence is in effect proof that God is dead, is quite faulted. In fact, to believe that we are the sole result of random explosions, unintelligent evolution, astroidal collisions, or a panspermic invasion leaves universal philosophies in a pile of hopelessness. Worse yet, that same ideology leaves humanity with a deeply troubling outcome in the context of disclosure—meaning a universe that is completely random implies that extraterrestrial morality without God must be equally random. This could mean that some of those little green guys (if that's what they are) might want what's best for us, while other creatures may want to eat us, using our throats as straws. This concept doesn't suit the extraterrestrial love of humanity philosopher because they are missing the logic, and the flaws in a non-God philosophy. If disorder is the law, we can expect consistent disorder, and that my friends will not bode well for humans if we engage with whatever and whoever is out there, especially if we're naively willing to bow before their magical, intellectual powers and supposed good will.

Fortunately, disorder is not what we observe here on earth or in space. Order is supreme. It's what keeps our planet spinning to the tune of 365 rotations a year. Order is characteristic of God. Disorder is characteristic of destruction, so if there is no God, there is no order. And if there is no God, and aliens are driving *them thar flyin' saucers*, we are at the mercy of random morality—random eating habits—random spirituality—random hunger pangs—

random sexual needs—and random meanings of hate, love, and empathy. In fact, all the nice ideas we have about aliens could be completely off if God does not exist, because an alien's concept of honesty could be completely random, as in honest about telling you what you want to hear because it suits the alien's needs, not yours.

That's randomness. That's the universe without God. That's a disaster.

With so much order in the universe, it is my belief that God will be acknowledged in universal philosophy (philosophy of beings outside of earth—if they exist) and that those that *do not* acknowledge Him will do so not because God does not exist, but rather, because we could expect innumerable attitudes much like people have here on earth—some might believe, some ignore, some resist, and others may hate or love God. Humanity may only be a small sampling of the potentially vast perceptions of God. This can be seen in the case of Luciferianism, where liberation from God is considered righteous and freeing. And this too, should not come as a surprise to the biblical scholar.

Going back to the order/disorder idea, I think it's safe to say that because these hypothetical peoples of the universe have not yet invaded us, they will never invade us. The reason I say that is simple: If they can get here today by way of dimensional transportation, they are light years ahead of us technologically and in their understanding of the laws of physics. If this is the case, they could've decided long ago to invade us—yet they haven't. They could have stripped us of our resources—but they have not. They could've genetically altered our DNA for our greater good millions of years ago—

and yet our genetic structure remains untainted. Therefore, I believe aliens will never invade us because if they were overcoming the obstacles of space travel to invade Earth, they would have taken our planet long before we poisoned it, long before we over populated it, long before we built massive armies with nuclear capabilities.

Why in the last 60+ years have UFOs become an increasing reality, versus the rare occurrence in the past? If they are so prevalent, why were they not the talk of every city in 1786, 1894, or 1921? And where were they when we didn't see them? My answer: They were always there. We can see this in cave drawings, writings, and rare artifacts—but they are rare because the beings behind the UFO phenomenon have always and continue to be *standoffish*, or as Enoch, that ancient man of God put it, they are *watchers*.

Why then do UFOs seem so prevalent today? The UFO experience is not new to mankind, it's simply taking on a new form, putting on a new mask, and adapting to a society that's been programmed to receive them.

I'd also like to point out that the craft recorded over time (at least 6,000 BC to present) seem to be advancing technologically and this presents a very serious problem for me. If extraterrestrials are so far advanced that they could overcome our known laws of physics thousands of years ago, then they would've been ions ahead of us technologically speaking. I think we all agree on that. These craft are capable of entering and exiting our physical existence—an obstacle not yet overcome by humans—at least not that the public is aware of. If that's the case, we're talking about a civilization gap that spans thousands, hundreds of thousands, or possibly millions of years. With that said, why were the aliens of 4,000 BC restricted to the archaic bell-shaped craft like the Vimanas recorded in India? Even if aliens were able to transverse time and space in the 1950's with the saucer shaped craft, why have they recently upped the ante to the ultra large and silent V shaped, contoured glossy black, or mirrored craft witnessed today? I call this the maturing saucer theory. And the theory agrees with Vallee's argument that these beings are presenting craft that fit the witnesses' cultural concept of advanced technology, or the highest level of imagined travel. This is why we see so many passages in scripture that correlate the flight of angels with blazing horses, balls of fire, and fiery chariots, passages that we will examine in detail.

Call the old saucer-style craft exhibit "A" if you like, but it seems to me that if extraterrestrials are crossing galaxies to get here, they would have refined their mode of transportation hundreds or thousands of years ago, not increased their technology in a matter of decades in a fashion that seems to be accelerating at the same rate as our own technology. My answer to this is: the entities behind the phenomenon adapt their deception to coincide with the cultures in which they present themselves, grandstanding as sovereign gods, benevolent caretakers, and aliens.

Balls of light, orbs, and glowing metallic balls (exhibit "B") are something altogether different. These are the prevailing "craft" on record and we'll spend a considerable amount of time on the specifics of these sightings.

~†~

If alien existence is a reality because life in all its forms is a product of random happenstance, we should expect a wide array of countless beings, of which the hungriest would have eaten us long ago. But we don't see that either. Abductees consistently report humanoid type life forms: Grey aliens, Reptilians, Tall Greys, and a few others. This coincides with the maturing saucer theory regarding the way aliens present themselves.

So if life in the universe is supposed to be random, how is it that aliens appear to have so much in common with our physical bodies?

In a recent announcement at the American Astronomical Society's 223rd meeting in January 2014, claims were made by researchers that life on the habitable planets in our solar system is likely to be much different than life on our planet because most of the inhabitable planets orbit red dwarf stars, which they assume will drastically change the appearance of life forms, if any exists, due to the drastic differences in sunlight, lack of spin, and variable tidal forces. Therefore, I have to conclude that since humans are still here living high on the proverbial hog, we are either alone in the universe, or the other beings, those random life forms that could easily consume or otherwise rape and pillage us, are held at bay by something, a force we cannot see. And that sounds like the God in the Bible.

I believe that if aliens exist, they are either under God's authority or His watchful eye. If that's true, a relationship could result between those who honor God, and a rebellion by those who resist. Again, this concept coincides with cross-cultural myths, and scripture, a pattern seen over and over between God, his creation, and angels both good and evil.

The Babylonian creation stories indicate that there was a disagreement between God (Ea), his son (Marduk), and the other deities regarding the position of man.[21] If the Babylonian tales reflect a hint of the biblical account, perhaps the fallen angels (the gods) did not want to serve humanity, but rather, to rule over us as indicated in the Isaiah passage. It seems to some degree that Satan and his fellow angels got their wish. Although according the Book of Job, they are still under God's sovereign authority, even after the fall.

"And there was war in heaven. Michael and his angels fought against the dragon, and the dragon and his angels fought back. But he was not strong enough, and they lost their place in heaven. The great dragon was hurled down—that ancient serpent called the devil, or Satan (the deceiver), who leads the whole world astray. He was hurled to the earth and his angels with him." (Revelation 12: 7-9)

"How you have fallen from heaven, morning star, son of the dawn! You have been cast down to the earth, you who once laid low the nations! You said in your heart, "I will ascend to the heavens; I will raise my throne above the stars of God; I will sit enthroned on the mount of assembly, on the utmost heights of Mount Zaphon. I will ascend above the tops of the clouds; I will make myself like the Most High." But you are brought down to the realm of the dead, to the depths of the pit." (Isaiah 14: 12-15)

"'You were the seal of perfection, full of wisdom and perfect in beauty. You were in Eden, the garden of God; every precious stone adorned you: carnelian, chrysolite and emerald, topaz, onyx and jasper, lapis lazuli, turquoise and beryl. Your settings and mountings were made of gold; on the day you were created they were prepared. You were anointed as a guardian cherub, for so I ordained you. You were on the holy mount of God; you walked among the fiery stones. You were blameless in your ways from the day you were created til wickedness was found in you. Through your widespread trade you were filled with violence, and you sinned. So I drove you in disgrace from the mount of God, and I expelled you, guardian cherub, from among the fiery stones. Your heart became proud on account of your beauty, and you corrupted your wisdom because of your splendor. So I threw you to the earth;'" (Ezekiel 28: 12-17)

Is this a historical record describing activity that took place on a distant planet somewhere far off in the universe? Or did an obscure race convince or deceive the writers of scripture, to make them believe that they were gods? Not likely. There is a clear pattern set forth throughout the Bible that God is Holy and righteous beyond our understanding, that He created all things on earth and the heavens, and that he created mankind, and the angels. Scripture is also very clear that God created angels with the *will* to choose right from wrong. And according to the Bible, Satan and his angels made a choice to rebel against God. And this clash in good and evil is still in existence, and experienced by humans every day on both a macro and personal level.

Jesus claims to have witnessed this act of rebellion when he was telling his disciples about the authority they would have over demons. He said,

"I saw Satan fall like lightning from heaven." (Luke 10:18)

Whether aliens are angels, demons, or extraterrestrials, Jesus clearly claims that he was present at the time of this heavenly fallout. Even Enoch claims that a Son of God, a Holy One, was present during his heavenly visitations, visitations often sited by ancient alien theorists.

If aliens from a distant planet convinced early humans that they were gods, as ancient alien theorists presume (taken from Zechariah Sitchen's work), you'd think they'd still be here, ruling over us, and that their wisdom about the vast universe would be an intricate part of our human experience. After all, aren't they supposed to be so advanced, so superior to us? Well, where are they now? Where are the gods from antiquity ancient astronaut theorists called the Annunaku? In my opinion, they are simply posing as something else. And maybe something worse—Aliens.

There are those, however, that suspect shape-shifting reptilian beings are quietly taking over the planet, unbeknownst to the populace. Although this theory is left to the furthest reaches of conspiracy theorists, some researchers such as David Icke take this idea very seriously. However, even if this theory is true, it can be ascribed to fallen angels because they can appear as men, beast, or craft—they truly are shape-shifting beings, capable to appearing as nearly anything as we will see in the forthcoming chapter. The Reptilian race is a common player among abductees' reports, found in cave paintings, and reported by UFO investigators including Bud Hopkins, among other high profile researchers. Could the Reptilians be connected to the race of fallen angels, the Annunaki, or remnants of the Nephelim? Did the fallen angels retain their intelligence, masking abilities, and dimensional travel after the fall? Or could the reptilian creatures reported by abductees be evidence that the "serpent" in the Bible was the very angel cast out of heaven, or something else altogether? Whatever the case, this may be a good time to ponder if there is a connection here to Satan, whose nickname is the "serpent" or the "great dragon", referenced over and over in Revelation 12 and 13. It seems the apocalyptic battle in the end times will be between Jesus and his angels, and the fallen angels led by that serpent, the great dragon, the "prince of this earth".

Could it be that our apocalyptic conclusion is a foretelling of a second heavenly battle between God's angelic hosts and what we call aliens? The vision Saint John recounts in chapters 12-20 culminates in this final chapter.

"And I saw an angel coming down out of heaven, having the key to the Abyss and holding in his hand a great chain. He seized the dragon, that ancient serpent, who is the devil, or Satan, and bound him for a thousand years. He threw him into the Abyss, and locked and sealed it over him, to keep him from deceiving the nations anymore until the thousand years were ended." (Revelation 20:1-3)

Although spiritual warfare is an unseen anomaly for the most part, what is apparent is that people experience good angels to this very day. We experience creepy supernatural events, and some undergo alien abductions, which often mirror the paranormal. All of these experiences reflect a clear line between good and evil—God and Satan. Not wishy-washy galactic randomness, but an intentional endeavor to harvest the souls of men. The ancient stories mirror modern narratives. The biblical tale in the garden reflects a reptile at odds with the Creator, and that in turn implicates today's consistent accounts of a "reptilian race" in abduction reports.

Going back to Vallee's supposition that whatever is going on is a dimensional phenomenon central to our planet or in a parallel dimension that exists all around us, we can deduce that all of these similarities are related thereby making the story marked out for us in scripture not myth, not a fairy tale, but an accurate account of what we know as a UFO universe. It may not be the universe some want to exist. But if we are living in a world filled with so many mysteries and unknowns, perhaps our reality is far more magnificent than we can imagine. Perhaps, those who have been subjected to the "alien" atrocities will receive justice one day, and maybe, if they seek out the God who watches over us, they will see His face, and they will enter heaven where there will be *"no more death or mourning or crying or pain"* (Revelation 21:4).

If these entities exist within our galaxy or the outer realms of space, and if we are remotely interesting enough for them to visit, study, or otherwise involve themselves with us in any physical way, the story of an alien/human co-existence would've ended long ago because the bending of time required for this to happen demands that their technologies would've overcome the obstacles of DNA and biological adjustments by now. Ten thousand years would be irrelevant, giving extraterrestrials the ultimate weapon—TIME—to rape and pillage us, so to speak, in a matter of seconds, and we'd never know what happened, or for that matter, that we ever existed. On the positive side, if aliens are all they claim to be, or all we hope they'd be, they could've altered our world for the better long ago as well. Again, this has not happened either. We are still living in the same "fallen" world as described in the Bible, a world whose only hope is in a patient, faithful Creator with an ultimate plan to renew and restore this broken world and repentant souls.

If aliens are real, they must be one of two things: either supremely good with limited human interaction, as evidenced by our existence, or they are evil and limited in their power by a God who monitors their interaction as well. I don't think the phenomenon has to be connected to one or the other. Why can't UFOs be related to both possibilities? Good angels and fallen angels. Both scenarios give evidence of a superior power source—God—and this, too, is shown over and over in the scriptures. The above passage from Revelation 12 continues:

"Then I heard a loud voice in heaven say: 'Now have come the salvation and the power and the kingdom of our God, and the authority of his Christ. For the accuser of our brothers, who accuses them before our God day and night, has been hurled down. They overcame him by the blood of the lamb and by the word of their testimony; they did not love their lives so much as to shrink from death. Therefore rejoice,

you heavens and you who dwell in them! But woe to the <u>earth</u> and the <u>sea</u>, because the devil has gone down to you! He is filled with fury, because he knows that his time is short.'"
(Revelations 12: 10-12)

If aliens are among us, and they have not obliterated us, saved our planet, or altered our DNA, they must want something else, something intangible, ethereal. Again, this corresponds with the biblical message. For the greatest commandment given by Jesus had nothing to do with money, science, physical possessions, technology, or natural resources. The Kingdom of God, according to the Bible, is first and foremost about captivating one's heart and soul. Jesus consistently preached this concept amid a people who were hoping for a military leader, a redeemer who would free them from the tyranny of Rome. Yet Jesus refused to give them what they wanted because God's Kingdom is not about human power and riches. The Kingdom of God is all about the soul; it's all about the spiritual experience; it's all about communion with God. This is illustrated in the following verses in which the Pharisees tried to trap Jesus by forcing him to choose a principle law, which was an impossible task in light of the labyrinth of laws the Pharisees and Sadducees thrust upon the Hebrew people, laws God did not give. As always, Jesus answers with wisdom and authority.

"'Teacher, which is the greatest commandment in the law?' Jesus replied, 'Love the Lord your God with all your heart, and with all your soul and with all your mind. This is the first and greatest commandment.'" (Matthew 22:37-38)

Jesus illustrated that he is from the kingdom of God after he healed a demon-possessed man, making the point that the kingdom is about the spiritual realm—not the earthly realm. When answering those who accused him of casting out demons by the power of Satan, he made the following statement:

"But if I drive out demons by the Spirit of God, then the kingdom of God has come upon you." (Matthew 12: 28)

Looking at the concept of extraterrestrial existence in a logical manner, it can also be said that there is a greater probability that we are connected, protected, and cared for by an intelligent designer simply by the realization that we still exist in contrast to alien domination. And yet as we look at the vast differences in morality, character, and belief systems here on earth, we can likewise assume that we do not live in a utopian universe, either. If the universe is teeming with life, we can further assume that the spiritual and moral differences between humans and aliens can be equally variable and unpredictable. Therefore, the spiritual battles that take place here on Earth, as discussed in scripture, must surely transpire in the heavens as well. With this as a possibility, I propose that if life exists on other planets, the God of the Bible is fully aware, and likely interacting with them, too. There is no evidence for this that I can find other than Ephesians 6:12 and a verse from Psalms 102:18. This verse is likely referring to those who would later be grafted into the Kingdom after the Messiah comes, but as in many verses we can infer the meaning to a larger scope.

"Let this be written for a future generation, that a people not yet created may praise the LORD..." (Psalm 102:18)

Alien Intervention

An example of what some believe to be alien intervention can be seen in the 1976 reports regarding UFOs shutting down missile silos at FE Warren AFB just west of Cheyenne, Wyoming. In this case, the military witnesses claimed that a bright, white pulsating light hovered over the silo, followed by the system uncharacteristically shutting down. The flying orb then moved on to other silos that shut down as well. After visiting multiple missile sites, the bright light shot straight up until it "looked like a star" and then disappeared. This happened again in 2010, and was witnessed by multiple military personnel and radar systems.

I will discuss how stories like these could be misinterpreted as alien intervention in the coming chapters. For now, it can be said with fair certainty that we are being watched, toyed with, and that we are under some kind of surveillance. This should not surprise the believer, and yet we are at risk of a complete aerial deception.

Likewise, in his zealous chase to understand the mysteries of the universe, the ufologist may be missing a bigger reality if he or she has already made up his mind about the nonexistence of God.

To this, I refer to Ephesians 6:12 once again.

"For our struggle is not against flesh and blood, but against the rulers, against the authorities, against the powers

of this dark world and against the spiritual forces of evil in the heavenly realms."

This passage clearly states that there are spiritual battles going on in the places we do not see. Fortunately, scripture addresses these battles from beginning to end, and provides insight and direction for this life and beyond. The authors and players on the biblical stage completely understood our supernatural reality. So why don't we? Modern humanity is either scratching their heads over these unidentified craft, skeptical, ambivalent, spiritually cold, or overzealous in making definitive claims.

In other words, we're lost. We're clueless about what's really going on up there. We want answers and we're grasping at little clues here and there, making assumptions based on our pre-established beliefs, and it's all getting washed into a bubbly mess of ideas. We want to understand what's going on in the universe at all costs. Some are even summoning whatever is out there, aliens, demons, creatures, or those little grey guys, hoping to make a spiritual connection with unknown beings they have never met and don't understand. Dr. Stephen Greer encourages this practice. He calls it C-5—this refers to a close encounter of the 5th kind—a mutually evoked encounter brought on via meditation, among other new age techniques.

Yikes! That sounds dangerous, especially if they don't know what they're conjuring. This is the same thing Crowley and others have done to invoke demons, and the same ideas practiced in ancient occults and satanic groups today. Is it any wonder there is evidence that fallen angels could be misrepresented in this story? Doesn't "extraterrestrial" sound much better than "demon" or "Lucifer"?

We may never unearth all the answers but I believe we can harvest a fair amount in the Bible. I will never concede that aliens do not exist. How could I? How could anyone make that assertion? We'll never fully know—at least not in this life. I do, however, believe we can get enough information from Scripture and other texts from antiquity.

When evaluating the National UFO Reporting Index posted on MUFON.com, I scanned the monthly reporting index and randomly chose to evaluate July, 2013. As it turns out, July 2013 had the highest number of monthly sightings ever recorded on the MUFON index, and the index dates as far back as 1561, recounting the Hans Glaser carving. I analyzed the July, 2013 index, searching for sighting reports that matched the biblical descriptions of angels that ranged from "star-like" qualities, balls of light, fireballs, and bright lights that exhibited the type of maneuvers described in scripture. I threw out almost all of the reports during July 3rd through the 5th because most appeared to resemble Chinese Lanterns even though they were believed to be UFOs. I also disregarded reports that included fireballs, bright lights, and star-like qualities if they were observed in a triangular, straight line, or possible structural formation.

After eliminating the non-applicable sightings, I found that out of 958 total UFO sightings during the month of July 2013, 421 matched the angelic descriptions found in the Bible. Less than 50 sightings were listed as disc shaped and after reading through the "disc shaped" reports I found that many actually described the UFO as a ball of fire and some even described a disc shaped object that later transformed into a ball of light. This information came as quite a surprise to me. After gaining a deeper understanding of angelic characteristics and abilities, this made perfect sense.

These statistics pointed me toward Jesus' place in the UFO universe, and they are critical in understanding why I believe Jesus is the central player. I'll get to this soon, but this is all very complicated and the unraveling process is going to require spelunking gear and shovels, because the secrets are buried very deep.

5.

DEMON DECEPTION

Many Christians unequivocally cast the role of aliens on Satan's minions—demons. At least this seems to be the most published theory coming from born-again Christians. Husband and wife writing team, Bob and Suzan Hamrick, discuss this traditional theory about aliens in their book, *Exposing Satan's Left Behind*.[22]

"All who are truly born-again are literally indwelt by the Holy Spirit, the third Person of the Holy Trinity. No one who is indwelt by the Holy Spirit can possibly be demon-possessed, much less transported to a demonic space ship for sexual relations, invasive "medical" procedures, etc., as have been described by many abductees of both sexes. What does this mean?

We find it remarkable that, of all of the reports of abductions by aliens, none seems to have been of anyone claiming to be a born-again Christian. If this is true, then it is the single greatest indication that "aliens" are actually demonic manifestations posing as extraterrestrial creatures. If the only people who can be abducted are those who have not accepted the Lord Jesus Christ as their Savior, and if no one who has accepted Him has ever been abducted, we have our answer to the mystery of 'space aliens'."

This statement points out an interesting idea—that these beings are demonic or something supernatural, multidimensional, and malevolent in nature. However, we could also assume that the creatures behind UFO abductions are simply nefarious beings from advanced civilizations or dimensions. If they are, and there is ample evidence that aliens are deceptive based on abductees' reports, then it will be difficult to gather accurate information about them, especially if they are prone to lying.

Could demons have a place in the UFO phenomenon? Sure. Could demons put on a mass deception by giving us visions of UFO craft, and alien abductions? No. God simply does not afford wicked spirits those types of powers, and there is no evidence that demons have the ability to create or convey the image of a craft, or coordinate a deception of global proportion such as the UFO phenomenon. They are submissive spirits, who obey Satan, their father, their master, and are subject to God's authority. There could be some truth in the demon deception, but I don't believe Bob and Suzan have connected all the dots.

In the abduction reports that I've read, the abductees religious beliefs were not always discussed. And there is a high probability that many abductees (like rape and molestation victims) fear shameful ridicule and the stigma that comes with victims of alien encounters, so they may never report their experience. There have been reports that abductions have stopped when abductees call upon the name of Jesus, but there have been reports that they don't, too. Could it be that using the name of Jesus alone is not enough? Or does there have to be a spiritual connection with that name—a soul connection—in order to stop the abduction?

It's impossible to prove the case that an ET is unequivocally demonic by citing the experience of a voluntary control group. One cannot declare that only non-Christians have been abducted because there are so few reports of Christian abductions. Besides, what Christian would say 'I was abducted by aliens' if the general consensus is that you can't be Christian and be abducted?

Because of these points, I will not claim that the UFO deception can *only* be related to fallen angels. I simply believe there are too many similarities to overlook the possibilities. Deception and malevolent activity certainly is key in many abduction cases. The fact that aliens have forcibly abducted humans in the middle of the night tells us about their ultimate respect for humanity. We will look at the demon deception in greater detail, but I think we need to gather some of the other pieces before the demon theory finds its place.

Public speakers and authors Joe Jordan, Chris Ward, and Guy Malone, co-founders of Alien Resistance, an organization dedicated to offering a biblical perspective on the UFO abduction phenomena, support and investigate the notion that demons and angels are behind UFO abductions. They train and educate Christian leaders in the "demonic deception". However, terminology is important here, so let me clarify; I wouldn't call UFO sightings demonic. From this point forward I will refer to any UFO sighting that matches the Bible's many descriptions of angels as an *angelic sighting*. These can be God's holy messengers, or a fallen angel. Demons are something altogether different.

I should also clarify that I do not believe that good angels are involved with alien abductions. God's holy angels sent to interact with humans never terrorized, or performed any kind of unwelcome procedure, although they were involved with creating life such as opening the wombs of barren women and the virgin birth. This, too, shows that angels were instruments used for genetic tampering indicating the possibility that the fallen angels would be interested in such activity.

We do not have enough information to delineate the abilities of good and fallen angels. Henceforth, I will describe the qualities given to ALL angels, fallen and good. It is these traits, along with biblical evidence, that connect Jesus to the UFO phenomenon.

Angels & Demons

Unfortunately, the Bible does not give many details about demons and their origins. We know they exist, but how they came to be and how they are connected to fallen angels is not definitively explained in scripture. One thing is for sure; the Bible does not state that demons are fallen angels. It appears this assumption is based on the evil nature displayed by demons, particularly in the New Testament. But there is a huge difference between the "spirit" nature of a demon, and the physical and spiritual nature of fallen angels.

I think this is an oversight by many Christians—believing that fallen angels were demons—because the Bible is very clear that one third of the angels followed Lucifer when he "fell" from heaven (Rev 12:4). That's a lot of angels, and a lot of power!

The Bible is also clear that hell is *reserved* for Satan and his angels at the final judgment (Matt. 25:41). Not all angels were bound in hell at the time of the rebellion. We see Satan traversing back and forth between heaven and earth in the book of Job, where he comes into the presence of God. As previously cited, Satan also interacted with Jesus in the desert, making it clear that he is still capable of traversing the earthly and heavenly realms.

"One day the angels came to present themselves before the Lord, and Satan also came with them." (Job 1:6)

"Then he showed me Joshua the high priest standing before the angel of the Lord, and Satan standing at his right side to accuse him." (Zecharia 3:1)

Clearly Satan, the fallen angel, still exists with his God-given qualities. He masquerades as beautiful and good, and is busy seeking to devour humans.

"And no wonder, for Satan himself masquerades as an angel of light." (2 Corinthians 11:14)

"Be alert and of sober mind. Your enemy the devil prowls around like a roaring lion looking for someone to devour." (1 Peter 5:8)

If Satan is free, who is in hell tormenting the lost souls? God had bound some angels and cast them into the pit/hell during what is called the second fall after the fallen angels corrupted themselves with the daughters of men (Genesis 6:1-1, 2 Peter 2:4). However, not all of the angels have been cast into hell just yet. Satan is free to roam in and throughout the earth, fully loaded with all of his spiritual powers and abilities (Job 1:6, Matt. 4:1). We see this all through scripture because Satan is actively involved in the world, as demonstrated in his visitation with Jesus in the desert among many other points of interaction.

So then where did the demons or demonic forces come from? There is only one source that I'm aware of that gives an indication where demons/evil spirits originated and how they are different from fallen angels: the book of Enoch. Referring to the Nephilim cited in Genesis 6:4, Enoch tells of a conversation with an angel regarding the Watcher's wicked offspring in Enoch 15:8-9.

"Now the giants, who have been born of spirit and of flesh, shall be called upon earth evil spirits, and on earth shall be their habitation. Evil spirits shall proceed from their flesh, because they were created from above; from the holy Watchers [fallen angels] was their beginning and primary foundation. Evil spirits shall they be upon earth, and the spirits of the wicked shall they be called. The habitation of the spirits of heaven shall be in heaven; but upon earth shall be the habitation of terrestrial spirits, who are born on earth. The spirits of the giants shall be like clouds, which shall oppress, corrupt, fall, content, and bruise upon earth."

This coincides with the testimony presented earlier by a member of a satanic cult that stated the fallen angels are still present in our reality.

"We worship spirits," he said, "we worship Lucifer and all his angels, and they're just as beautiful as before they were cast out of heaven."

Enoch makes it clear that evil spirits inhabit earth. He calls them "terrestrial spirits, born of earth". These are the ones who "oppress, corrupt, and bruise upon the earth". I'm not saying demons are not involved somehow in the alien deception as it relates to the terrestrial and paranormal aspects. Demons are spirit and cannot be seen unless they possess a body. However, from what we know about demons, they do not have the power to soar like stars, to manifest visions, or to transform their appearance. Their supernatural abilities are limited. Angels, however, are much more powerful.

It is a mistake in my opinion to classify fallen angels in the same camp as demons; they are clearly different in their abilities, characteristics, and freedoms. I think angels play an important role in the UFO universe where Jesus is concerned, so we need to be very clear when assigning roles to demons because they are very different from angels, fallen or otherwise. Demons are dark, unique spirits. Angels are a heavenly creation and far superior to demons. In my opinion, the demon/alien correlation is flawed because it leaves out obvious scriptural evidence, and ignores the documentation and military encounters as sighted in the Disclosure Project where high-level military personnel have encountered UFO's and allegedly witnessed fallen craft and survivors.

No matter what's behind the UFO and abduction phenomenon, I believe the demon-deception theory is too quick to dismiss the multitude of heavenly hosts. Furthermore, I cannot discount the existence of evil, spiritual, celestial, or dimensional beings involved in the abduction phenomenon. Something very powerful and intelligent is certainly at the root of these mysteries. But many UFOs seen in the heavens match the Bible's description of God's angels, so we *cannot* leave out the good ones like Michael, Gabriel, Raphael, and thousands of other angels that serve God on a daily basis. For they, too, are still interacting with mankind, still entering and exiting our existence in service to God Almighty. As we will see, fallen angels certainly fit the profile, too.

Fallen angels obviously exist in scripture, and according to the Bible and legends found in every culture, their work is visible in the evil that persists throughout the world. If fallen angels and good angels have the same powers to enter and leave our reality on demand, to soar at high rates of speed, have the ability to transform their appearances, and generate life-like dreams and visions, we can expect to see both types of angels actively soaring in the heavens, not just fallen angels. Experiencing the difference is only possible with an encounter—did the angel help, bring healing, a message from God, or usher a loved one into heaven? Or did the angel abduct, terrorize, and mistreat the individual against their will? These are hugely contrasting differences, but they are so common that I can't help wonder if we've mistaken a spiritual phenomenon with the UFO thing.

I won't dig into abduction research in this book because there are plenty of resources that examine this phenomenon. I will however, compare the abduction experiences with angelic encounters because there are many similarities. To get a better idea of what people are reporting about their abductions, I suggest reading *Masquerade of Angels* and *Taken: Inside the Alien-Human Abduction Agenda*, by Dr. Karla Turner, and *Abduction: Human Encounters with Aliens* (2009), by Dr. John E. Mack M.D. There are many more books that would make great resources, but these are a good start.

If all of this seems like fiction, it could be that our UFO universe is far more fiction-like or supernatural than we can imagine. After all, the universe is a very complex place, filled with surprises. With so many unknowns, shouldn't we be open to other possibilities other than what's been presented by the History channel?

When I began to seriously study UFOs, I realized the intelligence behind these unidentified objects function with an uncanny resemblance to the angels in scripture. They seem to be observing us like the "watchers" discussed in the book of Enoch, they are messengers, they come and go in the blink of an eye, they are powerful dimensional beings, they can change their appearance, they can be deceptive, and they are at war (spiritually speaking) among other attributes that we will discuss. As a result, I'm convinced that angels (both fallen and non-fallen) are at the heart of UFO encounters. Still, if they are angels, could the Messiah spoken of in the Bible be connected to the UFO phenomenon as well? After all, angels are messengers of God, and Jesus claims to be the Son of that same God.

I know all of this sounds strange. I cannot deny the spiritual experience of a believer, and in the same way I can't deny those who have experienced a UFO or abduction. I can, however, see how all of these experiences tie together, but only after studying the characteristics and abilities of angels.

People throughout history, and in our modern society, from every walk of life, claim to have experienced angels in tragic circumstances, in their greatest hour of need, or at their deathbeds. On a supernatural level, I think people in general have been more willing to believe in angels than UFOs. That may be changing. But have you ever wondered where the angels are before they make themselves known? I have, and here's what I found.

"The angel answered me, 'These are the four spirits of heaven, going out from standing in the presence of the Lord of the whole world.'" (Zechariah 6:5)

Many of the angels interacting with humans begin their journey in heaven. It seems that there are angels that regularly roam the earth, and there are those that come "down" here on special assignment. But we don't talk much about their travels, do we? Do they travel through time and space in the same way they did in Star Trek by using a "transporter" method, dematerializing and rematerializing as needed? Or do they actually travel at high rates of speed? Have you considered what their "approach" looks like when they enter our physical reality?

"About noon, King Agrippa, as I was on the road, I saw a light from heaven, brighter than the sun, blazing around me and my companions." (Acts 26:13)

"Each one went straight ahead. Wherever the spirit would go, they would go, without turning as they went. The appearance of the living creatures was like burning coals of fire or like torches. Fire moved back and forth among the creatures; it was bright, and lightning flashed out of it. The creatures sped back and forth like flashes of lightning." (Ezekiel 1:12-14)

Several individuals in the Bible experienced the UFO universe and it affected them in dramatic ways, usually pointing them to God, and inspiring them (at least for a time) to do great things. Now let's take a closer look at these UFOs seen throughout scripture. This is how the good angels interact. Based on what we know about Satan from the Book of Job, it is clear that he has a darker methodology.

Ancient UFOs?

According to ancient alien theorists, Elijah, a holy prophet in the Old Testament, was taken up to Heaven in a UFO, characterized as a "chariot of fire" in the account of Elijah's ascension described in 2 Kings. Elijah wasn't demon possessed, so this passage nulls the demon-only theory, showing that God was active in the UFO universe in the 9th century BC. However, the prophet did not encounter a physical craft as the ancient astronaut theorists assume. What he experienced was an angel.

If you watch Ancient Alien programs, you'll note their frequent mention that the prophet Ezekiel had a run in with a multi-wheeled thing-a-ma-jig in the sky. Upon further investigation, studying the passage in context, the object is clearly an angel—a cherub to be exact. Alien theorists use this one all the time, but like many "investigators" they grab whatever passage fits their premise, and claim it as evidence of alien craft without having a comprehensive understanding of angels, scripture, or the importance of reading in context when studying the Bible—and the Bible has much to say about the UFO universe if you are open to the seemingly hidden biblical perspective.

Another UFO incident frequently used by ancient astronaut theorists is Enoch's angelic encounter as found in the book of Enoch, a non-canonical text used frequently by the early church fathers and found in the Dead Sea Scrolls. According to this text, Enoch seems to have taken flight with some angels that gave him a tour of the heavens. Some theorize that Enoch went up in a space ship with aliens, and that his experience was misinterpreted as angels. Unfortunately, Enoch couldn't have been clearer that these entities were angels, holy servants of God, the creator of Adam and Eve and all that exists—not some set of "gods" from another planet. Where creation is concerned, Enoch assumes God is Creator of all there is. Clearly he does not see the angels as lower-case gods, or aliens from distant planets. They are the servants to the only God, the Lord of Glory.

"And as often as I saw I blessed always the Lord of Glory, and I continued to bless the Lord of Glory who has

wrought greatness of His work to the angels and to spirits and to men, that they might praise his work and all His creation; that they might see the work of His might and praise the great work of His hands and bless Him forever." (Enoch 36:4)

So the question remains; did the prophets encounter UFOs, or did they experience supernatural visions? Do their experiences align with similar angelic encounters?

Scripture is filled with what could appear to be UFOs, yet they are seldom demon driven. This is probably due to the fact that the authors engaged with God and his messengers more than they encountered Satan and his followers. The majority of biblical references to angels in scripture point to the good ones, if I may use that term. The Bible refers to the fallen angels on occasion in books like Genesis, Job, and Revelation, and other books like Enoch and Jasher. But we mostly learn about the appearance, gifts, and abilities of angels by studying the ones that were active in the Bible stories. One thing is certain, all angels, both good and rebellious, seem to have the same powerful qualities.

What's interesting to me is that both prophets (Ezekiel and Elijah) met with God and spoke on God's behalf, *and* encountered something that in a ET universe, would appear to resemble a modern UFO at a casual glance. So who was driving the "chariot of fire" and the "whirling-wheeled" craft Ezekiel encountered? Demons? Not at all. Angels? Yes!

Taking this a bit deeper, in 2 Kings chapter 2, Elijah went up in a "whirlwind". The word whirlwind translated in Hebrew is associated with being snatched away or some type of blast. But no matter how it is interpreted, young Elisha witnessed an event that evokes images of flying craft or some kind of time/space portal. This was not a demonic episode, nor was it a flying saucer.

As you will see scripture is not shy about addressing the appearance of angels in the sky, their approach, and their descent.

Angels are eerily similar to the most common type of UFOs—balls of fire or bright, star-like globes often seen zigzagging in the air. These are the same type of "craft" the famous 415th night fighter pilots called "Foo Fighters". In their initial report, which was taken very seriously by the military, WWII pilots described these UFO's as fiery balls of light that shone red, orange, or white. They were reported to be under intelligent control, and to take on military formations. They also moved at alarming rates of speed, doing impossible maneuvers, and then disappeared into the atmosphere.[23]

The military never came to a final conclusion, and the theories are not very substantial. One of the primary theories assumed the Foo Fighters were secret German weapons used to distract Allied pilots, and create troublesome electrical static. After the war, the Robertson Panel concluded that the Foo Fighters were not a threat, and that "If the term flying saucers had been popular in 1943-1945, these objects would have been so labeled."[24] Could this type of UFO, a typical fireball with "watcher" characteristics, be God's angels watching over our pilots in flight?

Are these objects mentioned in scripture? You betcha. They are called angels. They can have a metallic appearance depending on the type of angel, appear in multiple colors, and they are often referred throughout scripture as a horse, a chariot of fire, a horse carrying a rider, but they're most frequently called **stars**.

Angels are also called "host of heaven", and Satan's nickname is "the morning star". They zig. They zag. They enter this world in a whirlwind, perform military maneuvers, are compared to lightning, and as they manifest themselves into our reality, they transform from balls of light, to something like a blinding light, and finally into something that resembles a heavenly body with and without wings, a man, soldiers, or a physical craft of some kind.

We see this masking of appearances in the prophetic book of Zechariah. In the following passage we learn that angels take on the appearance of a physical craft, It makes sense that in antiquity one would have imagined a chariot when witnessing something soaring through mountain ranges. This is common when angels are in flight probably because there must be a transformation that takes place when they travel, and before they reveal themselves to men. This verse is most likely referring to the four winds, or four horsemen mentioned later in the book of Revelation—very powerful entities.

"I looked up again, and there before me were four chariots coming out from between two mountains—mountains of bronze. The first chariot had red horses, the second black, the third white, and the fourth dappled—all of them powerful. I asked the angel who was speaking to me, "What are these, my lord?" The angel answered me, "These are the

four spirits of heaven, going out from standing in the
presence of the Lord of the whole world. The one with the
black horses is going toward the north country, the one with
the white horses toward the west, and the one with the
dappled horses toward the south." When the powerful horses
went out, they were straining to go throughout the earth. And
he said, "Go throughout the earth!" So they went throughout
the earth. Then he called to me, "Look, those going toward
the north-country have given my Spirit rest in the land of the
north." (Zechariah 6:1-8)

Although scholars like to claim that these four horses and
four colors are representative of natural forces, it is clear that
they were sent from heaven to go throughout the earth as if
scouting out the condition of our planet. We know they
weren't really horses, because horses don't fly nor do they
come and go from God's presence into our reality. Angels,
however, do.

Angels are also called "spirits" (Zechariah 6:5). We know
that angels remain in God's presence, and that they come and
go according to God's will and pleasure. These four spirits
are very powerful angels who, according to the book of
Revelation, are given authority over the elements.

We see a physical angelic manifestation in Zechariah and
in the Elijah and Ezekiel accounts shown above. But we also
see this in the non-canonical book of Jasher, which is
mentioned in 2 Samuel 1:18, and Joshua 10:13. This book
was obviously read and trusted by the Hebrews because it
was cited in scripture. Chapter 71:9-11 details a
transfiguration, or delusion of mass proportions. In this

passage, Pharaoh discovers that Moses had slain one of the Egyptian foreman because of his cruelty. In this retelling that aligns with the Old Testament story, we see that angels can not only take on the appearance of physical craft, multiple objects and individuals, they can also project or transform into the image of someone else. These are very powerful abilities that I never imagined angels could possess. They were not used for malevolent purposes, only to protect the seed of the Messiah. Check this out...

"And Pharaoh heard of this affair, and he ordered Moses to be slain, so God sent his angel, and he appeared unto Pharaoh in the likeness of a captain of the guard. And the angel of the Lord took the sword from the hand of the captain of the guard, and took his head off with it, for the likeness of the captain of the guard was turned into the likeness of Moses." (Jasher 71: 9-11).

Incredible, isn't it? That angel sure was tricky. But that's not all that happened. The angel performs a supernatural function that duplicates what we see in the Book of Enoch and in abduction experiences today; he takes the hand of Moses and straightaway transports him to a distant location.

"And the angel of the Lord took hold of the right hand of Moses, and brought him forth from Egypt, and placed him from without the borders of Egypt, a distance of forty-days' journey." (Jasher 71:11)

We also see this in the New Testament when an angel

breaks Peter out of prison.

"The night before Herod was to bring him to trial, Peter was sleeping between two soldiers, bound with two chains, and sentries stood guard at the entrance. Suddenly an angel of the Lord appeared and a light shone in the cell. He struck Peter on the side and woke him up. 'Quick, get up!' he said, and the chains fell off Peter's wrists.

Then the angel said to him, 'Put on your clothes and sandals.' And Peter did so. 'Wrap your cloak around you and follow me,' the angel told him. Peter followed him out of the prison, but he had no idea that what the angel was doing was really happening; he thought he was seeing a vision. They passed the first and second guards and came to the iron gate leading to the city. It opened for them by itself, and they went through it. When they had walked the length of one street, suddenly the angel left him.

Then Peter came to himself and said, 'Now I know without a doubt that the Lord has sent his angel and rescued me from Herod's clutches and from everything the Jewish people were hoping would happen.'" (Peter 12:6-11)

Another amazing glimpse into the world of angels is found earlier in Jasher. In this passage we learn that angels can take on the appearance of more than one individual. In fact, they can materialize into a multitude of personalities. This passage truly shocked me.

"And the Lord heard the prayer of Jacob on that day, and the Lord then delivered Jacob from the hands of his brother

Esau. And the Lord sent three angels of heaven, and they went before Esau and came to him. And these angels appeared unto Esau and his people as two-thousand men, riding upon horses furnished with all sorts of war instruments, and they appeared in the sight of Esau and all his men to be divided into four camps, with four chiefs to them." (Jasher 32:27-29)

There is a clear difference in context when reading about the "horses" in the Bible. Horses were used as tools and weapons in terrestrial warfare, that much is obvious. This indicates that the writers of these ancient texts didn't just imagine that horses were flying about. When horses were on the ground, the author made it clear that they were walking on earth. But when they were sent from God to travel from heaven and throughout the earth, it is clear that this was a different context, and a different kind of horse. This is what I'm referring to when I advise reading scripture in the context of a UFO universe. Otherwise we can make wrong assumptions about the horses we're reading about— mammals, or angels.

I had to read the previous passage over and over because the implications are colossal. If angels can manifest an illusion of, or somehow generate the physical embodiment of multiple beings and weaponry, there certainly is reason to believe that UFO encounters and personal abduction accounts could be the same type of illusion, vision, or physical materialization found in the book of Jasher. It is this very type of physical and time-space manipulation Vallee discusses in his theories, and reported by those who have experienced the

UFO universe. And it seems the physical manifestations in the above passages are just as unidentifiable, and impossible to fathom as UFOs today.

Imagine the typical saucer-type craft with several beings looking through tiny portholes; this UFO, which probably appeared as a bright, star-like object at a distance, descends from the heavens, and presents itself in whatever form it desires, a metallic sphere, a ball of fire, a chariot, flying earthenware, or saucer. But could an object like that zigzags through the air, like many UFOs do, without completely shaking the passengers up like Saturday night margarita? No. Absolutely not. Again, this demonstrates that the extraterrestrial phenomenon is a faulted concept, excluding flesh and blood pilots and requiring a supernatural or dimensional entity at the helm of these craft. And the more evidence we find that angels can present themselves in whatever form they desire, including more than one object and humanoid entity, the more obvious it becomes that what we are seeing could be the work of angels—good or bad. The above passage in Jasher confirms that this phenomenon was experienced long before terms like UFO or extraterrestrial were even thought of.

As the passage continues, Esau and the angels exchange dialogue with these apparently flesh and blood warriors. And what is interesting to note is, there were 3 angels, and yet they could manifest into 4 groups of physically present soldiers sitting on top of horses and wearing armor, which is even more baffling. Yet in light of the seemingly impossible sightings, and abduction experiences today, it seems so very plausible.

This must sound absurd to those who disregard supernatural and UFO phenomenon. Still, the ufologist must take historical records like these very seriously because these stories mirror the very same phenomenon they are studying today. Moreover, the ancient astronaut theorist who uses passages from scripture and Enoch, should also take note of this possibility. The student of the Bible should also take the supernatural occurrences of antiquity into account in light of the many UFO sightings today. Surely there is a connection. It seems highly unlikely, to me, that these events that transcend thousands of years with incredible similarity are not related to modern experiences. For if stories like these are mythological fairy tales, than our modern society is living in a time of enchanted proportions.

The following passage further confirms that angels can take on the form of a flaming fire. I love Moses' reaction; it's so modern. His curiosity gets the best of him and he proceeds to boldly examine the sighting, hoping to make sense of that strange unidentified object.

*"Now Moses was tending the flock of Jethro his father-in-law, the priest of Midian, and he led the flock to the far side of the wilderness and came to Horeb, the mountain of God. There the **angel of the Lord** appeared to him in flames of fire from within a bush. Moses saw that though the bush was on fire it did not burn up. So Moses thought, "I will go over and see this strange sight—why the bush does not burn up."*

When the Lord saw that he had gone over to look, God called to him from within the bush, "Moses! Moses!" And

Moses said, "Here I am."

"Do not come any closer," God said. "Take off your sandals, for the place where you are standing is holy ground." Then he said, "I am the God of your father, the God of Abraham, the God of Isaac and the God of Jacob." At this, Moses hid his face, because he was afraid to look at God." (Genesis 3:1-6)

If the above passage is an indication of the power behind the intelligent pilots driving UFOs, there is no reason to believe that the alien-like inhabitants seen today could be as much of a "manifested presentation" as the angels Esau and Jacob experienced or those Enoch encountered in the next passage.

"And at that time the sons of men were with Enoch, and Enoch was speaking to them, and they lifted up their eyes and the likeness of a great horse descended from heaven, and the horse paced in the air. And they told Enoch what they had seen, and Enoch said to them, On my account does this horse descend upon earth; the time is come when I must go from you and I shall no more be seen by you.

And the horse descended at that time and stood before Enoch, and all the sons of men that were with Enoch saw him. And Enoch again ordered a voice to be proclaimed, saying, Where is the man who delighteth to know the ways of the Lord his God, let him come this day to Enoch before he is taken from us.

And all the sons of men assembled and came to Enoch that day; and all the kings of the earth with their princes and counselors remained with him that day; and Enoch then taught the sons of men wisdom and knowledge, and gave them divine instruction; and he bade them serve the Lord and walk in his ways all the days of their lives, and he continued to make peace amongst them.

And it was after this that he rose up and rode upon the horse... and it was upon the seventh day that Enoch ascended into heaven in a whirlwind, with horses and chariots of fire." (Jasher 3:27-32, 36)

What an amazing piece of literature. This excerpt is loaded with information and details that clarify that this encounter with a flying craft is connected to God and His angels. And once again we're told that these craft are perceived as horses and chariots of fire. Horses don't fly, so we know the angels either appeared as a horse and chariot, or Enoch was given a convincing vision. Is it any wonder the angels appeared as horses to ancient people? Horses and chariots were strong and mighty and associated with spiritual battle.

If you listen to the typical ancient astronaut theorist, you will hear about Enoch and his travels throughout the heavens in what is believed to be UFOs. Unfortunately, these researchers never mention Enoch's close relationship with the Lord, his interaction with angels, or his encounter with the pre-incarnate Messiah. He was very upright, and he truly lived a life worthy of his calling. No wonder he was allowed to soar with the angels and pass through heaven. The Bible gives us very little information about Enoch, which is too bad because there is much written about this ancient soul who walked with God for 300 years! The book of Enoch is very clear that God is the Creator of all things and that there is a Holy One who lives in His presence who is set aside to redeem all of humanity from their unrighteousness. Because of this, I'm saddened that the Book of Enoch was never canonized.

On the front end, it would seem as though these Enoch and the primitive men around him would have a difficult time comprehending such outlandish supernatural occurrences. I'm convinced, however, that they actually had a better understanding of who and what they were dealing with. They were connected with God in a unique way, in a unique time in history. And it is these carefully preserved and ancient accounts that lead me to believe that these God fearing men did not ignorantly presume that their fates rested in the hands of empty gods that blessed or cursed based on weather patterns, the success of crops, or natural phenomenon. Stories like the accounts I've presented give evidence that early man encountered supernatural entities with the means to travel in the air and through space-time. Moses in particular would live a life engulfed in the supernatural world that today would be labeled paranormal or extraterrestrial in nature. His earliest interaction with an angel can be found in the burning bush story. But God didn't stop there. Moses spent the rest of his life amidst miracles like rods turning into serpents, plague after plague afflicting the Egyptians, water turning to blood, the parting of the seas, pillars of fire and cloud, water pouring from rocks, and the food of angels falling to the ground year after year. These are all miracles attributed to God, but angels played an integral role, too, particularly the angel of the Lord. The angel of the Lord is the same one in the burning bush, the one who *has God's name in him*, and the one with power to forgive sins.

"See, I am sending an angel ahead of you to guard you along the way and to bring you to the place I have prepared. Pay attention to him and listen to what he says. Do not rebel against him; he will not forgive your rebellion, since my Name is in him. If you listen carefully to what he says and do all that I say, I will be an enemy to your enemies and will oppose those who oppose you. My angel will go ahead of you and bring you into the land of the Amorites, Hittites, Perizzites, Canaanites, Hivites and Jebusites, and I will wipe them out." (Exodus 23:20)

Many people are disgusted that God would have anything to do with murder, but the people he lists congregated with the fallen angel's offspring—the giants and the Nephilim, a corrupt and wicked race. Like all of mankind, angels have the free will to choose their own way, and many of them chose to rebel against the Holy One. That's just how God works. It's not a weakness; it's a strength, actually. Asking how God could let evil exist is like asking how children could ever love a parent that lets them learn by experience—it's like asking which is better, a gentle shepherd, or an abusive shepherd who beats his sheep into submission. In other words, no one likes to be forced to love their father, and fathers don't want to force their love on their children; doing so creates an environment of fear, a lack of trust, and is superficial. Bottom line: no one likes a micro-manager, and that is why everyone, including angels, is afforded *free will*—the will to choose. Of course, there are consequences to our choices. Isn't that what every good parent tells their children?

We'll take a closer look at the Nephilim later because their story is important, as well. The point here is that God continues to use his angels to protect the seed of the Messiah, and to rid the world of the remaining children of the fallen angels because they corrupted mankind before the flood, and were still around. Thus, the battle rages on.

I think our society has moved so far away from God in some respects that what used to be normal to those who walked with God—seeing angels zipping through the heavens—has become strange, taboo, or worse yet, "new age". God's messengers should never be taboo! The Bible invites us to pray for their coming, and especially for Jesus' return with his army of angels as prophesied in the book of Revelation. In doing so we usher in the ultimate destruction of the fallen ones, the dragon and all who follow him, those who thrive on chaos and darkness. Mindlessly conjuring unknown spiritual entities is not the same; that's a dangerous and foolish undertaking. Therefore, it is critical in understanding the difference between God's team and the fallen team.

"Dear friends, do not believe every spirit, but test the spirits to see whether they are from God," (1 John 4:1)

This is so important. God's word serves as protection from the "lie". It is a weapon against the deceitful beings that are mistreating us. Fallen angels are intelligent, powerful, and deceiving creatures bent on stealing your soul from God. And this is where they use demons; to manipulate the world of those they are pursuing. If you study abduction cases you'll learn that paranormal activity is a secondary part of the experience. Not only does the victim undergo an abduction or vivid UFO sighting, they later encounter objects moving in their homes, or other fearful paranormal activity, including ongoing psychic communication with a spiritual entity that, for whatever reason, reinforces the messages communicated in the abduction experience. Thus,

"The Spirit clearly says that in later times some will abandon the faith and follow deceiving spirits and things taught by demons." (1 Timothy 4:1)

Do not abandon the faith, but rather, grow your faith, knowing that we live in a universe that is supernatural in nature and that the powers within it are at war for our souls. The following two chapters will present a very detailed case that UFOs are most likely angels based on the biblical descriptions given to these powerful entities, both good and fallen.

6.

ANGEL FIRE

Compare the Foo Fighter descriptions with an angel and you will be shocked. The resemblance is awesome. Interestingly, the nickname military pilots once used for altitude is *angels*, as in "Angels Fifteen" means 15,000 feet.[25] The term is no longer in use, but I wonder if there is a connection? Whether angels have a historic link to aeronautics or the famed Angel's Rest hiking trail in Oregon, we are about to discover a list of compelling characteristics UFOs share with these spiritual beings. The evidence for angelic UFOs may provide an explanation not only for these strange lights, but actually point us to a battle taking place in the heavens and in the hearts of men—the only battle that Jesus concerned himself with. And as we follow the angel fire, we'll see that they could also be related to the abduction phenomenon, as well.

It's easy to overlook angels as a possible UFO explanation because of their commonly preconceived appearance, and misunderstood and unbelievable origination. Although incorrectly portrayed as little chubby babies with wings, they are much more powerful, multidimensional, brighter, and appear in numerous shapes and sizes from man-sized to very tall. In fact, in recent years the Internet has exploded with reports of angel sightings and encounters.

One story in particular stands out in my mind. The story can be found everywhere on the web, and featured on the 700 Club. Christine Martin lost control of her car one day until it finally came to rest, hanging over the edge of a bridge. Then while she dangled there, she claims that a huge angelic being that must've been at least 50 feet tall, "huge in stature", picked up her car, moved it from the edge of the bridge to safety. This experienced changed her life and drew her to God—the premier goal of good angels.

I know that others have had similar experiences. Stories like this not only demonstrate the supernatural, and the love of God, they also indicate how powerful these beings are and how dissimilar they are to the traditional angelic concept. I believe our false perception about angels and their appearance has caused many to overlook their place in the UFO universe.

Scripture frequently refers to angels as "stars". In fact the Bible has many names for angels including, but not limited to, "heavenly hosts", the "heavenly array", and "starry hosts". Although these phrases may be used on occasion to describe the constellations, there are several passages where the term "star" is directly correlated with angels. The Book of Daniel expresses this definitively in a passage referring to the coming anti-Christ, found in chapter 8: 9-10.

"Out of one of them came another horn which started small but grew in power to the south and to the east and toward the Beautiful Land. It grew until it reached the host of

the heavens, and it threw some of the starry host down to the earth and trampled on them." (Daniel 8:9-10)

Angels are also described as "stars" in Revelation 12:4,9, Job 38:7, and Matt 2:2. They are probably called stars because they shine so brightly, and because they take on a star-like appearance when moving *in and throughout the earth*. Angelic "stars" are also mentioned in Judges, referring to their involvement with spiritual warfare, and in Revelation 1:19 when Jesus explained John's vision.

"From the heavens the stars fought, from their courses they fought against Sisera." (Judges 5:19)

"The mystery of the seven stars that you saw in my right hand and of the seven golden lamp-stands is this: The seven stars are the angels of the seven churches, and the seven lamp-stands are the seven churches." (Revelation 1:19)

We see this in Jude, too, showing that both the good and fallen angels are referred to as stars. This tells us that the starry hosts we see in the sky can be both good, possibly swooping down to help someone in need or see them off to heaven, or in the case of the fallen ones, entering our reality to deceive and destroy. Jude tells us of the angels destined to eternal damnation.

"They are wild waves of the sea, foaming up their shame; wandering stars, for whom blackest darkness has been reserved forever." (Jude 1:12)

I think it's pretty cool that God calls angels "stars". It's endearing, appropriate, and telling. God gave them a nickname that characterizes their appearance, brilliance, purity, and incredible power. This name alone should be enough to cause us to take a second look at their place in the UFO universe.

So how do we know which "stars" are good and which are evil? There's a big difference in the way fallen angels interact with humans compared to the good ones. Those who have encountered good angels are usually drawn to God. However, fallen angels can *appear* to be good (Corinthians 11:13-15). Over time, encounters with an evil spirit or elementals can develop into a dark presence or a lying spirit. Eventually, the truth comes out.

"And no wonder, for Satan himself masquerades as an angel of light." (2 Corinthians 11:13-15)

"You said in your heart, 'I will ascend to the heavens; I will raise my throne above the stars of God; I will sit enthroned on the mount of assembly, on the utmost heights of Mount Zaphon.'" (Isaiah 14:12-14)

Beyond explaining what happened in the heavenly realms between God and Lucifer, this verse also shows that there could be many more verses where the term *star* refers to angels when we would otherwise think it is talking about the constellations. In this verse, the term stars could refer to Lucifer's desire to rise above the constellations, but that seems absurd considering that vastness of the universe. It makes much more sense that Satan wanted to rise above all the angels (stars) and rule over them as God rules over them.

~†~

On the bright side, angels can also take on a female form. I have read modern day accounts where witnesses believed they encountered a female angel, and this seemed odd to me. I didn't remember reading about female angels in the Bible. But then I found a passage, and maybe the only verse, that delineates a female angel.

"Then I looked up—and there before me were two women, with the wind in their wings! They had wings like those of a stork, and they lifted up the basket between heaven and earth." (Zechariah 5:9)

Another point to consider is that the Hebrew term for "host" when used in the angelic context means *army*.[26] I doubt the author was talking about an army of stars as in burning spheres of hydrogen and helium. In Strong's Hebrew Dictionary, the Hebrew usage for *host* refers to an army, military force, or band of soldiers.[27] This certainly sheds some light on how the writers of the scripture experienced these creatures—a far cry from flying toddlers. Angels can enter and leave our reality in the blink of an eye. They can be seen approaching earth with the appearance of a star, and can shoot straight up from the earth and disappear as they leave our atmosphere.

Most people are familiar with good angels, the type that we are most familiar with—those who help us—those who serve God's creation—and those who communicate with us on God's behalf. There are also angels of the fallen variety. They are not demons. They are the angels who rebelled against God; you know the ones—the angels that followed Lucifer (Satan) and were consequently cast out of heaven. Some were bound in the "pit" according to scripture, Hebrew legend, and the book of Enoch. And although most people believe Satan resides in hell, most of the fallen angels are still at large, still have their angelic powers and characteristics, and are still rebelling against their Creator. Why would they stop? They're doomed no matter what they do.

A better question would be, wouldn't they ramp up their rebellion as the day of their damnation draws closer? And where have they been all these years since the days of Christ? Exactly what have they been up to? They are eternal beings, so they've had plenty of time to polish their master plan. Perhaps we're still watching it unfold to this very day.

If you've experienced a UFO first hand, or if you've watched some of the eyewitness videos showing these bright balls of light we've named UFOs, you'll recall that they are often seen in a group, and can take on military formations. A perfect example of this is the shape the Arizona lights formed when hovering above the Arizona sky in 1997, creating a large "V" shape in the night sky. A military formation is very common in videos where we see balls of light soaring in the heavens, turning on a dime, each ball independent, yet moving in sync with the others in a playful, intelligent manner. This is not always the case; some large groupings of UFOs operate without an organized pattern, but there is no doubt that many clusters of UFOs are interconnected somehow, or intelligently assemble their formations.

The military formations can stir fear in those who witness their presence, and there may be good reason for this if the angels are of the fallen variety. But should we really fear these unidentified objects? According to scripture, we are told that angels are most definitely operating in our reality and that they enter in and throughout our world, both in service to God and in rebellion. We see this in the book of Job. Although we don't know for sure when this book was written, we can safely say that it was penned after Satan's fall from grace. The forthcoming passage clearly demonstrates that Satan himself, along with other angels, are still allowed to travel in and out of the heavenly and earthly dimensions.

"One day the angels came to present themselves before the Lord, and Satan also came with them. The Lord said to Satan, 'Where have you come from?' Satan answered the Lord, 'From roaming throughout the earth and going back and forth in it.'" (Job 1:6-7)

If you've watched UFOs zipping around the sky, the words "roaming throughout and going back and forth" definitely seem to characterize the strange coming and goings these objects are associated with. Their movements don't always make sense if they're entering our atmosphere to perform scientific studies or looking for a place to land. On the other hand, a biological and dimensional entity with personality paints a different possibility.

The Bible tells us that we're not living in a world dominated only by what we see, but rather a world where we are at odds with spiritual forces interacting with, and influencing the affairs of the *powers*, *principalities*, and *authorities* in the heavenly realms—all names given to the ranks of angels.

The battle for our souls should be evident to us all. One turn of the page in our history books reveals evil on many fronts. Headlines are riddled with bad news reflecting the evil that is so prevalent in the world we live in. But the media also bears witness to the good and righteous moments that give us hope. There is good reason for this eternal clash that we call good versus evil—a theme I've used in all my fiction, an essential element when framing the human condition. We are at war, spiritually speaking, and this is why I featured the following passage from Ephesians at the beginning of this book:

"For our struggle is not against flesh and blood, but against the rulers, against the authorities, against the powers of this dark world and against the spiritual forces of evil in the heavenly realms." (Ephesians 6:12)

What does this passage mean? It simply means that there is a spiritual battle going on here among the rulers and authorities in the *heavenly realms*—or the sky above that we see, and the space we cannot. And nowhere else is this more prevalent than in our skies, where UFOs are on the rise.

Some of the best UFO researches have concluded that the UFO phenomenon has been around since the dawn of mankind. They have documented the existence, appearance and descriptions of our planetary visitors, and yet we are still bewildered by them no matter how much data we gather. Yet as the UFO reality stirs our imaginations in our modern world, with all our gizmos and technologies, it is critical to understand that these visitors and their means of traveling to and from their place of origin is found, with ample evidence, in the books of the Bible and other books deeply rooted in the Judeo/Christian library.

Outside of Christianity, Berosus, priest of Bel-Marduk, wrote a Babylonian history in Greek in 250 BC, passing on ancient secrets. He wrote about the creation story, including monsters that are strikingly similar to what we might imagine a fallen cherub looked like. Could this affirm the creation process and the angelic fall from heaven?

"There was a time in which there existed nothing but darkness and an abyss of waters, wherein resided most hideous beings, which were produced on a two-fold principle. There appeared men, some of whom were furnished with two wings, others with four, and with two faces. They had one body but two heads..." [27b]

The ufologist should certainly take note of these passages, because the Bible gives these beings/unidentified objects the credibility they deserve. They are not "space junk" or "swamp gas" or "weather balloons" according to the Bible. According to God's Word, they are exactly as the viewer experienced, intelligently driven, watchful and curious, entities of a heavenly origin. The creatures mentioned by

Berosus in the above text is a perfect match to Satan's profile—he is a cherub, and cherubs have 4 wings. So what were these creatures roaming through the darkness and the abyss of early creation? I believe they were Fallen angels.

The difference between the scientific evaluation of UFOs and the biblical account is that the authors of scripture do not disregard the phenomenon; they wrote it like they saw it. You have to get this. The Bible does not negate or refute our UFO universe. Scripture does not disregard UFO sightings because God is the source of their existence, author of their movements, and designer of their destinies.

Have we mistaken the UFO phenomenon's place in our theologies and catechisms? Yes, I believe we have. But if the reader believes that UFOs and God cannot co-exist, it is clear that that is a wrong assumption; for it is God and His Son who command these "stars" to ascend and descend upon the earth. Whether the reader chooses to believe God is divine or an extraterrestrial being with grandiose self-given authority makes no difference; the Bible is absolutely clear about the source of these bright, metallic, fiery whirling wheels. Whether the reader chooses to examine the Bible in the context of a UFO universe is yet another choice. However, because the Bible presents such vivid descriptions of intelligent and powerful beings soaring in and out of our reality—the same descriptions set forth by modern UFO witnesses—it seems to me that in all of its historical accuracy on many other counts, we can only gain confidence in the Bible's connection to our modern world, and in the message within its pages. If ever there was a time to appreciate the Bible—the Living Word, it is now—a time when spiritual battles are raging hotter than ever, a time when angels are making themselves known right before our very eyes.

7.

ANGEL DNA

In 1537, a group of villagers from Franconia saw a large, star-like object coming from the sky. As it approached the townsfolk, it looked like "a large white circle from which whirlwinds and patches of fire came forth."[27c]

Could it be that what we witness in the heavenly realms today is the very activity that the Ephesians 6:12 passage speaks of? Perhaps the terrestrial battles that took place between the Hebrews and the Mesopotamian kingdoms and their successors had less to do with power and wealth acquisition, and more to do with the battle between heavenly and evil forces as discussed in scripture.

If you read the many passages that mention the host of heaven in context, you will see the Bible is often referring to angels. Studying these passages will give you an increased sense of who and what is soaring above us, and why they interact on our behalf. Knowing what scripture has to say about these beings gives us a better idea why they are here, and paints a clearer picture that remarkably resemble the UFOs we see today.

Angels, the "Stars" of the heavens

In the following passage, Isaiah describes a vision he has regarding the fall of Babylon. In this passage, God shows Isaiah that Babylon will fall in the same fashion as Satan. Lucifer, the fallen angel is referred to as the "morning star, son of the dawn" and the other angels that Lucifer (Satan) aspired to rule over are also called stars.

"You said in your heart, I will ascend to heaven; I will raise my throne above the stars of God; I will sit enthroned on the mount of assembly, on the utmost heights of the sacred mountain. I will ascend above the tops of the clouds; I will make myself like the Most High." (Isaiah 14:12)

This passage caught my attention because the lights thought to be unidentified objects, are often seen near mountain ranges, flying around in glorious fashion, soaring at will, often as if they're up there simply to display their abilities above the clouds, with no logical flight pattern.

Apparently Isaiah was given insight into the events that took place in heaven, including the very words that Satan uttered, if not audibly, quietly to himself. Of all the angels, he should've known that not a word is spoken without God knowing. Therefore, either the angels or God's spirit revealed the intentions of Satan's heart to the prophet to help him understand what the human race is up against.

And what are we up against?

We stand against a powerful angel who desires to rise above the throne of God, to be seen as creator, to replace God. He would not submit to God, let alone mere mortals sentenced to work the filthy earth because of their own sins. He was too proud for that. Satan wanted to be seen above the heavens, recognized as one who soars above the mountains, to literally be viewed as a superstar, one that would be worshiped as greater than God Almighty. Thus, the morning star was cast out of heaven, eternally separated from God with a fixed sentence, eternal damnation into the lake of fire, and temporarily bound to earth with exceptions allowed only by God.

Luciferians take this very seriously. To them, Lucifer (Satan) is a rebel of the highest order, the ultimate "free thinker", and he is worshiped to this very day.

It is often wrongly assumed that Satan resides in hell. He does not, although it has been prepared for him. Until then, he is free to roam, free to soar above the heavens, free to pretend that he is a god, prince of this world, and as Ephesians 2:2 states, *"ruler of the kingdom of the air"*.

As Satan's time comes to an end, it only makes sense that he will become increasingly active as Christ's return looms over his ever-failing mission. Likewise, we would expect to see increased angelic activity *against the powers of this dark world and against the spiritual forces of evil in the heavenly realms* as the return of Christ draws nigh. And with so many star-like "craft" soaring in our skies, it's no wonder he is called ruler of the kingdom of the air. What else could that statement mean?

Angels seen as bright lights, fire, torches.

In the following passages we read Ezekiel's initial vision of the Cherubim as they approached him near the Kebar River.

He paints a detailed picture of what he witnessed. Ancient alien theorists almost unanimously use this story to describe a UFO encounter, but the Hebrew prophets were very familiar with Cherubs because the image of two golden Cherubim were carved, plated with gold, and mounted over the Ark of the Testimony. But in this passage, Ezekiel sees the cherubim descending to earth as they brought him a vision of the throne of God—an experience that must have been exhilarating to say the least.

Note that when the Cherubim are in the clouds, they enter in a "windstorm", a term frequently used when angels are present. They look like "brilliant light", "fire", and in the center he sees "glowing metal". This passage also alludes to a military formation when it states that their "wings touched one another" as they move through the clouds, a common modern-day UFO observation.

"I looked and I saw a windstorm coming out of the north—an immense cloud with flashing lightning and surrounded by brilliant light. The center of the fire looked like glowing metal, and in the fire was what looked like four living creatures. In appearance their form was that of a man, but each of them had four faces and four wings, and their wings touched one another.

Each one went straight ahead; they did not turn as they moved. Their faces looked like this: Each of the four had the face of a man, and on the right side each had the face of a lion, and on the left the face of an ox, each also had the face of an eagle. Such were their faces. Their wings were spread out upward; each had two wings, one touching the wing of another creature on either side, and two wings covering its body. Each one went straight ahead. Wherever the spirit would go, they would go without turning as they went.

The appearance of the living creatures was like burning coals of fire or like torches. Fire moved back and forth among the creatures; it was bright, and lightning flashed out of it. The creatures sped back and forth like flashes of lightning." (Ezekiel 1:4-14)

The passage continues with the "wheel within a wheel" terminology. I find this particularly interesting, not that it represents a "flying saucer", but that the wheel imagery certainly puts a physical stamp on the Cherub's appearance, and demonstrates God's creativity. But make no mistake; Ezekiel clearly sees these things as living creatures, created by God. The reader may also note that modern UFO sightings are frequently seen amidst lighting, and where multiple spheres flash out of a single ball of light... *Fire moved back and forth among the creatures.* To the ufologist, this type of activity should sound familiar. And the casual Youtube watcher has likely viewed many videos capturing this exact type of UFO activity.

In another passage located in chapter 10, Ezekiel explains that these are cherubim, not "star ships", or any type of craft, but a very specific brand of angel.

"When the living creatures moved, the wheels beside them moved, and when the living creatures rose from the ground, the wheels also rose. Wherever the spirit would go,

they would go, and the wheels would rise along with them."
(Ezekiel 1:19-20)

This passage could explain why some angels are often referred to as a rider on a horse and a chariot of fire as found in Isaiah's account in 2 Kings, and other biblical verses. But look at the following passage in Chapter 10 when Ezekiel calls these things what they are. The four-faced, four-winged creature is also mentioned in Revelation when John describes the throne of God in Revelation 4:6-8. The context is clearly referring to the angels and "elders" encircling the throne, worshipping God. So any concept that the Ezekiel encounter is anything but an angel is simply flawed.

"I looked, and I saw beside the cherubim four wheels, one beside each of the cherubim; the wheels sparkled like chrysolite. As for their appearance the four of them looked alike; each was like a wheel intersecting a wheel. As they moved they would go in any one of the four directions the cherubim faced; the wheels did not turn about as the cherubim went.

The cherubim went in whatever direction the head faced, without turning as they went. Their entire bodies including their backs were completely full of eyes, as were their four wheels. I heard the wheels being called 'the whirling wheels'. Each of the cherubim had four faces: One face was that of a cherub, the second the face of a man, the third the face of a lion, and the fourth the face of an eagle.

Then the cherubim rose upward. These were the living creatures I had seen by the Kebar River. When the cherubim moved, the wheels beside them moved; and when the cherubim spread their wings to rise from the ground, the wheels did not leave their side. When the cherubim stood still, they also stood still; and when the cherubim rose, they rose with them because the spirit of the living creatures was in them." (Ezekiel 10:9-17)

Talk about a close encounter. No wonder UFOs can turn in any direction and hover in place! No wonder so many of these fiery balls of light seem intelligent—they are powerful creatures whose spirit dwells within an object that is both physical and supernatural. It makes perfect sense that Jacques Vallee has concluded that UFOs are too supernatural to be nuts and bolts craft.

These racing balls of light (orbs) are extremely common with UFO encounters, and this is especially true where they are seen hovering, and then making impossible maneuvers. And it doesn't matter how big or small the account; angels can easily manipulate their size and appearance. The Ezekiel account sounds like the 1606 sighting in Kyoto, Japan when a "whirling ball of fire resembling a red wheel hovered near the Nijo Castle."[27d] In this case, could the samurais have witnessed a cherub and its whirling wheels?

Another point to consider in our angelic investigation is the consistent multi-dimensional factor that accompanies UFO encounters. Angels are from heaven, and no one really knows where that is located. Most people I've talked to assume heaven is located somewhere within another dimension. And so when we see UFOs coming from nowhere and disappearing into thin air, we can assume that these objects are also multi-dimensional in the same way Vallee's data proves. In addition, there is much debate whether a physical nut-and-bolt structure can actually tolerate inter-planetary/multi-galactic space travel without mortal damage to the craft and its passengers, making dimensional travel a more likely scenario.

The truth is, we can't understand how flesh and blood life forms could survive long distance travel in a ball of fire, or a glowing metallic craft sometimes seen dripping metallic globules. This is clearly beyond our available technology. Even those who have seen these bright, starry craft in a C3 (close encounter of the 3rd kind) do not have any idea who or what they are dealing with. Angels, however, fit this description of most UFO sightings because they are spiritual beings (Hebrews 1:14) with powerful, "blazing" capabilities.

"This will happen when the Lord Jesus is revealed from heaven in blazing fire with his powerful angels." (2 Thessalonians 1:7)

It's helpful to compare the biblical point of reference when we consider that the majority of UFO encounters are balls of light, flaming circles, and brightly lit circular or orbed shaped objects. Jacques Vallee affirms this with his massive library including thousands of case files.[28] This tells us that the angels from heaven were just as real to the authors of scripture as they are to today's witnesses. Apparently, both ancient and modern men are experiencing the same psychic or supernatural phenomenon, whether the connection is heavenly or something else.

Remember the Foo Fighters? They were the balls of colored light that circled around WWII fighter planes that were "not a threat". In cases like this, it's almost as if the UFOs are not mechanical in nature, but rather, personal, intelligent beings genuinely interested in human activity. And this is reminiscent of the four horses described in Revelation, Ezekiel, and Jasher.

Do you remember reading the statement by Don Philips from Skunkworks? With the above Ezekiel passage fresh in your mind, here's a portion of what he said:

"I looked up in the air and saw these objects, lighted objects, moving at tremendous speeds. But right at the instant when I saw these things making acute angles and traveling, eh maybe I would estimate, three to four thousand miles per hour, and then immediately making a acute turn, I knew they weren't ours. I'm thinking what kind of forces these uh, if they were people in these craft, what kind of forces their bodies are taking. And I said, 'Well these have to be guided by some type of... intelligent pilot, if you will. And then all of a sudden, they seemed to group from what would be hundreds of miles in the sky to the east or to the west and they came into a circle, rotated in a circle and disappeared... As far as the inhabitants thereof, we don't know."

Well, maybe we *can* know whom the inhabitants are if we pay attention to what God has shown us in scripture.

- **"What kind of forces their bodies are taking?"** Angels are heavenly bodies and spiritual beings, therefore the laws of physics may not apply because of their supernatural nature. Based on the biblical description of angels, this explains the crazy maneuvers, speed, and collective conscious exhibited in their ability to "group" together from hundreds of miles apart.

- **"They have to be guided by some type of intelligent pilot."** Angels are extremely intelligent, spiritual creatures. They are heavenly hosts created to serve God, worship him, intimately familiar with God's ways, and to interact with man on his behalf as it applies to God's greater plan.

- **"Rotated in a circle and disappeared."** They are dimensional. They engage with us in physical and spiritual form. Some are ascribed with whirling wheels, or wheels within a wheel.

- **"As far as the inhabitants thereof, we don't know."** True. We don't know and we may never know unequivocally, but scripture draws a pretty good case that many of these intelligent pilots could be angels.

Cherubs are interesting creatures, but they are only one of the many types of angels. The seraphim have six wings (Isaiah 6:2), and although the popular representation paints all angels with wings as seen in the many statues around the world, some do not have wings at all and some can look just like men (Genesis 19:1-5). There are also Archangels,

Thrones/Ophanim, Dominions, Virtues, Erelim, Elohim, Bene Elohim, Powers, Authorities, Principalities/Rulers, and Angels. Here are a few passages that show that some angels appear as men:

"I looked, and I saw a figure like that of a man. From what appeared to be his waist down he was like fire, and from there up his appearance was as bright as glowing metal." (Ezekiel 8:2)

"While I, Daniel, was watching the vision and trying to understand it, there before me stood one who looked like a man. And I heard a man's voice from the Ulai calling, 'Gabriel, tell this man the meaning of the vision.'" (Daniel 8:15)

"They raised me up into a certain place, where there was the appearance of a burning fire; and when they pleased they assumed the likeness of men." (Enoch 17:1)

If angels can look like men, a flaming fire, a horse or chariot, they can appear as anything! Perhaps the idea of angel wings was birthed from their aerial encounters. Maybe we see them as they are, or as we imagine. Maybe they allow us to see them in the manner acceptable to the viewer. Wings or no wings, there is no doubt that the Bible references these fiery entities.

One of my favorite characters, who eventually earned his wings, is Clarence from the classic movie, *It's a Wonderful Life*. But he, too, is a false representation of God's angels because people don't become angels and they don't earn wings. It is only upon the return of Christ that the redeemed will "shine like stars" (Daniel 12:3). Scripture tells us that angels were made to be messengers, servants and worshipers of God, and servants of men according to God's direction. They do not accept worship and they do not encourage the worship of stars, the moon, or any of the constellations—unless they are fallen (Revelation 19:10).

Here are some additional angelic characteristics:

- Angels are created to serve God (Psalm 148: 2-5, and Colossians 1:15-16)

- Angels were created long before man (Job 38: 6-7)

- Some angels rebelled against God (2 Peter 2:4)

- Angels travel back and forth throughout the earth (Job 1:6-7)

- They are ministering spirits (Hebrews 1:14)

- God makes angels like the wind, flames, and fire. (Hebrews 1:7)

- Angels submit to Christ (Colossians 1:16)

- Angels are not to be worshiped (Colossians 2:18)

- They are extremely powerful beings (Acts 12:23)

- There are thousands upon tens of thousands of angels, and one third of them were cast out of heaven (Revelation 5:11)

- There are ranks and orders of angels (Daniel 12:1, 1 Thessalonians 4:16, Colossians 1:6)

Similarities between Angel and alien visitations:

- A bright light precedes interaction. *"About noon as I came near Damascus, suddenly a bright light from heaven flashed around me. I fell to the ground and heard a voice say to me, 'Saul! Saul! Why do you persecute me?'"* (Acts 22:5-7)

- Visitation is usually associated with some kind of paralysis, fear or terror. *"As he came near the place where I was standing, I was terrified and fell prostrate. 'Son of man,' he said to me, 'understand that the vision concerns the time of the end.'"* (Daniel 8:17)

- The witness is often told to not be afraid. *"But the angel said to them, 'Do not be afraid. I bring you good news that will cause great joy for all the people.'"* (Luke 2:10)

- Visitations are accompanied by vivid visions. *"And behold a dream came to me, and visions appeared above me."* (Enoch 13:9)

Many abductees recall walls or ceilings opening up as if it were dematerializing before their eyes. One such account is documented in the Ted Rice account in *Masquerade of Angels*. In that account, we read, "He didn't argue with her. Like him, both Amelia and Marie had seen the walls or ceiling dissolve and vanish, and they had encountered non-human creatures in unknown craft."[29]

- <u>Abductees are lifted and taken up, in what is often described as an out of body experience, to a place that appears to be real</u>. *"They elevated me aloft to Heaven."* (Enoch 14:10).

  "In my former book, Theophilus, I wrote about all that Jesus began to do and to teach until the day he was taken up to heaven... After he said this, he was taken up before their very eyes, and a cloud hid him from their sight. They were looking intently up into the sky as he was going, when suddenly two men dressed in white stood beside them. 'Men of Galilee,' they said, 'why do you stand here looking into the sky? This same Jesus, who has been taken from you into heaven, will come back in the same way you have seen him go into heaven.'" (Acts 1:1, 9-11)

Non-canonical references to angels:
- The First Gospel of the Infancy of Christ 3:3. Although this text is ascribed to James and generally read by the early church, it was not canonized, but the texts speaks of angelic "stars" as an accepted term.

"And at the same time there appeared to them [the wise men] an angel in the form of that star which had before been their guide in their journey; the light of which they followed till they returned into their own country."[30]

- The Gospel of the Birth of Mary 7:4-5. *"But the Virgin, who had before been well acquainted with the countenances of angels, and to whom such light from heaven was no uncommon thing, was neither terrified with the vision of the angel, nor astonished at the greatness of the light, but only troubled about the angel's words."*[31]

Angelic "star" qualities:

- Judges 5:20 – *"From the Heavens the stars fought, from their courses they fought against Sisera."*

- Job 38:7 – *"...while the morning stars sang together and all the angels shouted for joy?"*

- Isaiah 14:12 – *"How you have fallen from Heaven, morning star, son of the dawn".*

- Luke 2:13 – *"Suddenly a great company of the heavenly host appeared with the angel, praising God, and saying, 'Glory to God in the highest Heaven',"*

- Revelation 12:4 – *"His tail swept a third of the stars out of the sky and flung them to the earth."*

- Revelation 18:1 – *"After this I saw another angel coming down from heaven. He had great authority and the earth was illuminated by his splendor."*

- Matthew 2: 9 – *"After they had heard the King, they went on their way, and the star they had seen in the east went ahead of them until it stopped over the place where the child was."*

- Revelation 9:1 – *"The fifth angel sounded his trumpet, and I saw a star that had fallen from the sky to the earth. The star was given the key to the shaft of the abyss."*

- Revelation 9:17 – *"The horses and riders I saw in my vision looked like this: Their breast plates were fiery red, dark blue, and yellow as sulfur. The heads of the horses resembled the heads of lions, and out of their mouths came fire, smoke and sulfur."*

Who are these horses, and riders on horses? They are warrior angels, the same who will come with Jesus in the clouds, and cited in many passages throughout the Old and New Testaments. Clearly Jesus's return is going to be very noticeable, and will take place in the air. We see this confirmed in Matthew Chapter 24:

"For as lightning that comes from the east is visible even in the west, so will be the coming of the Son of Man... 'The sun will be darkened, and the moon will not give its light; the stars will fall from the sky, and the heavenly bodies will be shaken'... At that time the sign of the Son of Man will appear in the sky, and all the nations of the earth will mourn. They will see the Son of Man coming on the clouds of the sky, with power and great glory. And he will send his angels with a loud trumpet call, and they will gather his elect from the four winds, from one end of the heavens to the other." (Matthew 24: 27, 29-35)

In my opinion, the heavenly bodies falling will not be the constellations seen in outer space. I think the dimensions that separate our reality and the heavenly realms will literally be "shaken", disturbing whatever separates us, causing the angels, and/or other beings traversing these dimensions to be fully exposed. At that time Jesus will be accompanied by the heavenly hosts, his heavenly army will be revealed, and the judgment will commence.

Angels were viewed from the perspective of the witness so when the men of antiquity had no other reference point for travel, it's easy to see why they would assume the fire balls approaching earth in a whirlwind would appear to be chariots of fire or riders on a horse—they had no other point of reference. Today, we see something else. But when we put the pieces together, we can see that all of these have much in common.

"...a chariot of fire and horses of fire appeared and separated the two of them, and Elijah went up to heaven in a whirlwind". Elisha cries out, *"Father! The chariots and horsemen of Israel!"* (2 Kings 2:11)

Where else do we see this whirlwind associated with angels and chariots? In Ezekiel 1, the angels come in a windstorm. In Hebrews 1, the author tells us, *"...he makes his angels winds, his servants flames of fire."* This is also mentioned in Isaiah, Hosea, and in the book of Jeremiah the author writes,

"He advances like the clouds, his chariots come like a whirlwind, his horses are swifter than eagles." (Jeremiah 4:13)

Notice the repeating reference to airborne phenomena like the clouds, wind, whirlwind, and eagles soaring. We can imagine that angels are strictly beautiful winged creatures that suddenly appear in a bright light, but as seen in the above passages, they serve a greater purpose and can be seen in the sky as UFO-type bright lights. They soar around the earth. They fight spiritual battles, sometimes going out as an army of angels. They perform aeronautical displays that rival the famed Blue Angels, and all of this has been in the pages of the Bible for thousands of years.

Why have we not discussed this? Why is this not part of our doctrines? Without this knowledge, we know very little about the work angels do and how they get it done and what they look like when they enter our reality.

Angels are Princes of heaven and earth:

Angels are not only referred to as stars, horses, and chariots of fire; titles that denote their abilities—warrior—traveler—powerful. Angels are also called "princes", particularly when they are associated with spiritual matters, or when they are extremely powerful. Some of the angels with this title are Michael, Gabriel, Uriel, and Jesus—the Prince of Peace.

"But the prince of the Persian kingdom resisted me twenty-one days. Then Michael, one of the chief princes, came to help me, because I was detained there with the king of Persia." (Daniel 10:13)

"But the Pharisees said, 'It is by the prince of demons that he drives out demons.'" (Matthew 9:33-35)

Jesus was given a princely title, which further leads me to believe that he is *"the angel of the Lord"* spoken of in the Old Testament.

"God exalted him to his own right hand as Prince and Savior that he might bring Israel to repentance and forgive their sins." (Acts 5:30-32)

"For to us a child is born, to us a son is given, and the government will be on his shoulders. And he will be called Wonderful Counselor, Mighty God, Everlasting Father, Prince of Peace." (Isaiah 9:5-7)

The angel of the Lord:

The angel of the Lord is certainly a unique angel. He takes on specific responsibilities, has a unique authority that differs from other angels, and can appear as a flame or bright light.

"There the angel of the Lord appeared to him in flames of fire from within a bush. Moses saw that though the bush was on fire it did not burn up." (Exodus 3:1)

I also noticed a previously mentioned verse associates Jesus with the same qualities as an angel when Saul (who later is named Paul) encounters the spirit of Jesus Christ. The verse demonstrates that an angel-like being approached Saul, and yet the voice was that of the resurrected Christ, who Saul was persecuting inadvertently by killing Jesus' followers. Is this further evidence that Jesus is the angel of the Lord, the earthy manifestation of God Almighty?

"About noon as I came near Damascus, suddenly a bright light from heaven flashed around me. I fell to the ground and heard a voice say to me, 'Saul! Saul! Why do you persecute me?'" (Acts 22:5-7)

In addition to serving as the voice (word) of God, the angel of the Lord is a mighty warrior. He carries a sword and slays the wicked in righteous anger. Passages like these make non-believers cringe, sometimes turning them away from God. But the angel is not painted as a murderer, but a righteous, Holy judge with authority to arbitrate the deeds of men, not because he wants to kill or punish according to human understanding, but because he is HOLY and punishes wickedness, a concept that is nearly impossible for people to understand in this day and age.

"In his right hand he held seven stars, and coming out of his mouth was a sharp, double-edged sword. His face was like the sun shining in all its brilliance." (Revelation 1:16)

"David looked up and saw the angel of the Lord standing between heaven and earth, with a drawn sword in his hand extended over Jerusalem. Then David and the elders, clothed in sackcloth, fell facedown." (1 Chronicles 21:15-17)

"I turned around to see the voice that was speaking to me. And when I turned I saw seven golden lamp stands, and among the lamp stands was someone like a son of man, dressed in a robe reaching down to his feet and with a golden sash around his chest. The hair on his head was white like wool, as white as snow, and his eyes were like blazing fire. His feet were like bronze glowing in a furnace, and his voice was like the sound of rushing waters. (Revelation 1:12-15)

Beyond communicating the word of God and revealing mysteries, the angel of the Lord protects, avenges, and delivers his people.

"The angel of the Lord encamps around those who fear him, and he delivers them." (Psalm 34:6-8)

The angel of the Lord spoke with Moses, and called himself "I AM"—as Jesus called himself before the Jews (John 8:58). This is a very strong statement, and infuriated the Jews so much that they crucified Jesus because of it. Calling himself I AM was nothing short of blasphemy; a name the Jews recognized as the name God gave himself when speaking to Moses from within the burning bush. But if you remember, that passage places the angel of the Lord within the bush and credits him as God:

"There the angel of the Lord appeared to him in flames of fire from within a bush." (Exodus 3:2)

The way this verse is phrased causes me to believe that it was the angel of the Lord who was actually speaking from within the bush, not God the Father, doubly affirming that Jesus was the angel of the Lord, and that Jesus is equal with God.

~†~

With everything the Bible tells us about angels, I am thoroughly convinced that most of the unexplained balls of light seen in the sky, misidentified as Foo Fighters, UFOs, and alien craft, are indeed angels. I believe these are the starry hosts recognized throughout scripture, and posted in artwork over the course of time as colorful spheres, balls of fire, and the lights that take on military formations. As stated repeatedly throughout scripture, they are involved in spiritual matters here on earth and in the heavenly realms.

It is because of this spiritual battle that I believe the biblical descriptions of angels, and their similarity to UFOs has been kept from the UFO hobbyist. The evil one, who masquerades as an angel of light will do anything to keep humans from believing that God exists and that God loves all of creation. It is the evil one's ultimate desire that no one put his or her trust in God, especially Jesus Christ.

The determination aliens have to move us to a higher spiritual plane is an old trick, copied straight from Satan's playbook first used in the Garden of Eden.

"Here, eat this and you will become like God," hissed the serpent.

Today, the fruit we are given is UFO encounters, but the message the aliens are presenting is essentially the same—you can become spiritually advanced—negating God's supremacy. This is exactly what the Bible says the serpent told Eve, only in slightly different terms.

"You will not certainly die," the serpent said to the woman. "For God knows that when you eat from it your eyes will be opened, and you will be like God," (Genesis 3:4-5).

So she ate the fruit, but did she become like God? No. And if we listen to the aliens, will we be like God? No. The lie remains the same, as predicted in 2 Thessalonians. And this is the message Satan has tried to communicate since the creation of man, a message regularly reported from abductees.

~†~

Good angels show up in traumatic circumstances, save lives in miraculous ways, and visit the bedsides of the sick and dying. Thousands of people around the globe acknowledge their presence. Doctors hear of these stories on a daily basis. Accident survivors tell of angelic beings in the form of men, children, and winged helpers, some similar in size to humans and some very large, catching them as they fall, pulling them from dangerous circumstances, and otherwise protecting them from harm. Try a Google search and you'll read the never-ending saga of angels impacting humans across the globe everyday as we struggle through life and at our deathbeds. And the visitations are increasing each year.

Guess what else is increasing every year? UFOs.

The National UFO Reporting Center has reported that UFO sightings jumped by 42 per cent between 2011 and 2012. This could be a sign of the times or a result of the vast amount of media coverage the phenomenon is getting nowadays. Either way, sightings are increasing.[32]

We can only imagine how they've interacted on our behalf, how many lives they've saved, and how many near misses were altered by their presence. On the other hand, the devastation that fallen angels and demons have caused is equally apparent.

It's a travesty that we see angels only as unidentified flying objects and extraterrestrials, although that is what they may be. Could our inability to recognize their true identity be the real deception? Is our confusion a result of the spiritual warfare Paul spoke about in the book of Ephesians? Have we fallen prey to the lie already?

"For this reason God sends them a powerful delusion so that they will believe the lie." (2 Thessalonians 2:11)

Scripture makes it very clear that the lights and starry hosts in the heavens represent both sides—good and fallen angels. This should give us cause to fear the power that truly exists within these beings, but more importantly, the God that created them. Their presence gives us hope and their existence tells us that we are protected from and at battle with a force at odds with God almighty. For as it says in Romans 8:31, *"If God is for us, who can be against us?"*

Isn't this the answer so many are hoping to glean from extraterrestrial beings—that we are not alone, that we are cared for, and that we are protected from forces of evil? Thankfully, this is the very premise we find within the Bible.

There is more we can learn about angels like their ranks, their names, and the types that exist, but the fact that angels are here and that they are interacting with us, is not the point. Angels are only guest stars in this monumental performance played out on the world stage.

With the introduction of angels, the warriors in the heavenly realms, we are getting closer to introducing the star of the show, the "bright morning star", not to be confused with the "morning star, son of the dawn". We cannot discuss angels without studying them in the context of Jesus Christ because they are dependent on God and His Son, and exist solely to serve the Godhead; for Jesus is the "Lord of hosts" and master of the fiery show in the heavens. And we cannot discuss Jesus without first analyzing the qualities of angelic creatures. Angels do his bidding, and serve him in the battle of righteousness, a war that started long ago, long before we occupied God's creation and the place where Satan and the fallen ones dwell. So if we are to study his place in the UFO universe, we have to understand exactly where he fits and why he is the principle player. He far exceeds Robert Redford, Ben Affleck, and Clint Eastwood on this stage. He is the leading actor, director, and producer of what will be the greatest show on Earth, and what we are seeing in the skies is only the beginning of what is to come.

Like many believers, I've marveled at the idea of God's place in the supernatural. I love angel stories and have always been eager to know more about their interaction with us, not only in scripture but in modern testimony as well. So it wasn't until I did a serious inquiry that I observed a honest-to-goodness connection between the UFO phenomenon and angels, which then led me to question how Jesus fits in as well.

The concept of angels as UFOs can lead one to believe that the aliens of today are the angels written about in scripture; the very beings represented on cave drawings, amulets, and Phoenician artifacts. The characters in these types of evidence are marked with stars, wings, and celestial bodies, as well as occult symbology, "scorpion" and reptilian bodies. If we interpret these representations as "extraterrestrial" it is easy to believe that the only option is to interpret modern UFOs as visitors from other planets.

One could then assume that the same must be true of Jesus—that he was an alien. But let me be clear—I'm not saying that. There is no evidence to support such a theory. Jesus and his angels have nothing in common with the conduct of aliens described by abductees. History and scripture credits Jesus as a Hebrew of Hebrews. Although scripture claims that he was man in body, and God in spirit, there is never any indication that he was non-human. Likewise, the angels described in scripture are spiritual and very powerful, never taking on the form of 4-foot tall grey men from Mars.

What I am saying is that these airborne beings were active and evident among the Jewish people and all other cultures throughout time. And to take it one step further, Jesus himself was well aware that angels existed and that they soared in and out of our existence. He explicitly stated that angels will join him when he comes back to finish the work he started. He was also very clear that Satan has come to "steal and kill and destroy" (John 10:10).

8.

THE BATTLE

Ancient alien theorists present classic works of art that display UFOs at war, battling in the clouds, bright spheres and dark balls engaging in aerial battles thousands of years ago. Some abductees return with frightening, fearful experiences, and those who encounter UFOs are left awestruck by the sight of the hovering objects above. We can see that something is going on, even in classic art, but is it really spiritual in nature? Well, can anyone argue that the human race is at odds with one another? Governments are dripping with corruption, some conducting genocide; teens are killing each other in school, major conflicts erupt daily, not to mention the individual corruption in our hearts and minds.

I recently watched a news report from Central Africa in which a man called "Mad Dog" was literally eating a man's heart out, and it wasn't his first cannibalistic act. History repeats itself as they say, but with all of our worldly wisdom and scientific advancements, you'd think we'd successfully applied our knowledge to create peace on Earth, but that is not the case. Every day there are new wars and rumors of wars.

If aliens from other planets have been visiting us over the course of time to help us spiritually, as some theories go, they haven't helped much. In fact, it seems like violence and war are increasing across the globe. On the other hand, what we are seeing is exactly what the Bible has predicted all along—a spiritual battle between God and his fallen angels that will eventually get worse and worse, and ultimately culminate in the clouds, a heavenly battle that will put an end to the "Dragon" who is the deceiver, the evil one, the "ruler of the air", and the "prince of this earth". Therefore, a UFO universe should not surprise the believer because it was predicted thousands of years ago. And who knows how far the spiritual battle extends... to earth... to Zeta Reticuli... to the far reaches of the cosmos? To your very heart?

In reference to Jesus, Paul gives us some insight into Christ's place in this battle. Every battle has a leader. Satan leads rebellious angels and demons. But Jesus leads the heavenly hosts. Therefore, if we give any thought that the bright balls of light that enter our world are angels we must include Jesus in the discussion. Paul, an adopted Apostle, preached that Jesus was God. Paul was a devout Jew who at one time encouraged the murder of Christians for their blasphemy, but later, after encountering the risen Christ, repented and preached that Jesus was the actual Son of God, the prophesied Messiah—a major turnaround. Here's what Paul said about Jesus when he wrote to the Ephesians about this Christ.

"He who descended is the very one who ascended higher than all the heavens, in order to fill the whole universe." (Ephesians 4:10)

Fill the whole universe? With what? Peace? Forgiveness? God's Love? And why is that? Why is Jesus necessary, and what does he have to do with UFOs? As far as humans are concerned, he is necessary to conquer sin and to end the ongoing battle between the evil that has corrupted all of creation, including the fallen angels. And here in Ephesians we see that his purposes extend beyond earth into the *whole universe*. I can speculate about that idea, but I won't. This passage leaves us with more questions, and although it can lead to an exciting conversation about the extent of God's free gift of salvation, I'll leave the theorizing over that verse to C.S. Lewis.

In terms of spiritual warfare, I haven't read any passages in scripture that indicate a battle other than the one in our terrestrial world and the extraterrestrial battles that occur in the heavens. The war could be more astronomical than we can imagine. Who are we to limit God's definition of the *heavens* and who are we to limit his measurements of the *whole universe*. If angels can move throughout our reality with so little effort, I imagine they can go to other realms and galaxies to serve as needed. We can't fathom how these entities move through space and time because it is simply beyond our scope of understanding, but make no mistake, angels have crossed over into our terrestrial existence since the beginning of time.

If you struggle with the concept of spiritual warfare and God's place in such work, simply consider the atrocities that have occurred throughout history and you will quickly be reminded how evil this world can be, and how desperately we need God's love and intervention. Consider Hitler's attempt to exterminate the Jews, the Khmer Rouge Regime, Rwandan genocides, Roman Catholic sex abuse, The Crusades, Ted Bundy, Nero, Javed Iqbal, Jim Baker, Jeffrey Dahmer, Andrei Chikatilo, and I could go on. To assume that humanity is generally good is naïve, a false concept of the world we live in, a mistaken understanding of the evil that dwells in the hearts of men. The Bible is very clear that evil is at play on a universal scale and in the recesses of the human heart. It is also plain that in the end, God will overcome, he will heal all wounds, and each of us will have our day in court.

We can't always see the spiritual battles taking place in the heavens. Too often we do not even recognize the spiritual battles raging in our own minds. This battle is clearly understood by Paul, the author of Ephesians, and it was most certainly acknowledged by Enoch, Ezekiel, and Elijah. And maybe, if we can accept the testimony of those who report UFOs across the world, we might find it logical to accept the testimony from our brethren in the past who logged their encounters with these spiritual forces—God's angels who represent both sides of the "extraterrestrial" encounters, the good ones who have done nothing but protect and guide us, and those who seek to perform intrusive and traumatic medical experiments and sexual acts (as reported by abductees) against those they claim to serve.

~†~

By taking a closer look at the "Heavenly Army" that serves God's righteous purposes, we will see that these beings are not a long lost mythical race created in the minds of misguided Neanderthals. Angels are real and numerous. They are powerful. They are watching, and they are for us. However, there are some that are not acting in our best interest—some that hate and want to devour us—hence the battle.

We are fortunate to find a snapshot of spiritual warfare in 2 Chronicles 18:18-20 where it reads,

"And the Lord said, 'Who will entice Ahab, king of Israel into attacking Ramoth Gilead and going to his death there?' One suggested this, and another suggested that. Finally a spirit [another term for angel] came forward, stood before the Lord and said, 'I will entice him.'" (2 Chronicles 18:18-20)

In context we know that Ahab had done wicked things in the sight of the Lord, so God was cultivating the affairs of men, while at the same time, punishing Ahab for his wickedness.

We are given another example of angels involved with spiritual matters within the book of Daniel. This scene follows a series of prophecies and visions, which we will look at later because what Daniel experiences over and over is eerily similar to those experienced by abductees—bright lights—angelic visitations—vivid, life like visions. In verse 4 he describes the angel:

"I was standing on the bank of the great river, the Tigris. I looked up and there before me was a man dressed in linen, with a belt of the finest gold around his waist. His body was like chrysolite, his face like lightning, his eyes like flaming torches, his arms and legs like the gleam of burnished bronze, and his voice like the sound of a multitude..." (Daniel 10:4)

And then in verse 12, the angel says,

"Do not be afraid, Daniel. Since the first day that you set your mind to gain understanding and to humble yourself before your God, your words were heard, and I have come in response to them. But the prince of the Persian kingdom resisted me twenty-one days. Then Michael, one of the chief princes, came to help me, because I was detained there with the king of Persia. Now I have come to explain to you what will happen to your people in the future, for the vision concerns a time yet to come." (Daniel 10:12)

The angel proceeds to instruct Daniel about the coming Messiah, and details an apocalyptic prophecy. Daniel writes,

"At that time Michael, the great prince who protects your people, will arise. There will be a time of distress such as has not happened from the beginning of nations until then. But at that time your people—everyone whose name is written in the book—will be delivered." (Daniel 12:1)

The prophetic sequence ranging from Daniel 10:12 substantiates the spiritual warfare taking place in the heavens, and how God's angels have and continue to interact on our behalf. This interaction is apparent in the book of Zechariah. Chapter 1 details one of Zechariah's eight visions:

"During the night I had a vision—and there before me was a man riding a red horse! He was standing among the myrtle trees in a ravine. Behind him were red, brown, and white horses. I asked, 'What are these, my lord?' The angel who was talking with me answered, 'I will show you what they are.' Then the man standing among the myrtle trees explained, 'They are the ones the Lord has sent to go throughout the earth.' And they reported to the angel of the Lord, who was standing among the myrtle trees, 'We have gone throughout the earth and found the whole world at rest and in peace.'" (Zechariah 1:8)

Are you getting this? Angels, frequently characterized as horses, angels of the fighting variety, go throughout the earth, observing our behavior, flying throughout the heavens in multi-colored objects that the author interpreted as horses because he knew of no other means of transportation. These angels are probably in the same category as those that appear as chariots of fire, or the riders on horses described in the book of Revelation. They could also be the UFOs and balls of light we see taking on military formations. This makes perfect sense because their report indicated that they were scanning the earth for wars, or the potential for war, but found peace.

These angels remind me of the UFOs that interacted with the nuclear launch sites mentioned earlier. They also remind me of the famed UFO that disabled a rocket traveling several thousand miles per hour in 1964 as reported by Dr. Bob Jacobs, former 1st Lieutenant in the US Air Force. In this case, a test missile was launched, and during the launch, a UFO was recorded flying with and around the missile and disabled it with a beam of light. This event was videotaped and witnessed by several military personnel.

We see angels interacting on man's behalf in Elijah's experience, in the book of Psalms, and in the book of Isaiah. Each passage references "chariots" in a military context. This is further evidence that this type of angel is geared for battle, poised to protect, and very powerful.

Sometimes angels travel alone, and other times they enter as a pack, much like Kenneth Arnold's 1947 sighting near Mt Rainier.

"Then the Lord opened the servant's eyes, and he looked and saw the hills full of horses and chariots of fire all around Elisha." (2 Kings 6:17)

"See, the Lord is coming with fire, and his chariots are like a whirlwind; he will bring down his anger with fury, and his rebuke with flames of fire." (Isaiah 66:15)

"The chariots of God are tens of thousands and thousands of thousands." (Psalm 68:17)

If you've witnessed a UFO, these scenes may appear eerily familiar. But the more important things to consider are why these chariots of fire and flaming angels are revealed in scripture, what they are, and who is directing these angelic missions. In the Zechariah 1:8 account, the angels are sent by God, and report to the *angel of the Lord*, the leader of that particular spiritual reconnaissance. And this is just one of many verses in which Jesus, the alleged angel of the Lord, interacts with men in a UFO setting. So if God has an army of angels—the heavenly hosts—and they report to the angel of the Lord, thought to be the pre-incarnate Messiah, then this angel must be the Admiral of the fleet. Jesus' position as *Great Admiral* [name created by me] is not only shown here in the Old Testament, it is also very clear in the New Testament.

"There is no one like the God of Jeshurun, who rides across the heavens to help you and on the clouds in his majesty." (Deuteronomy 33:26)

"He makes the clouds his chariot and rides on the wings of the wind." (Psalm 104:3)

Throughout the New Testament, Jesus refers to himself as the Son of Man, a name used in the Book of Daniel that the Hebrews understood to mean the Messiah. The following passages refer to the Son of Man as he comes on the clouds in power and authority to judge all of creation.

"In my vision at night I looked, and there before me was one like a Son of Man, coming with the clouds of heaven. He approached the Ancient of Days and was led into his presence." (Daniel 7:13)

"Then will appear the sign of the Son of Man in heaven. And then all the peoples of the earth will mourn when they see the Son of Man coming on the clouds of heaven, with power and great glory." (Matthew 24:30)

"Jesus replied. 'But I say to all of you: From now on you will see the Son of Man sitting at the right hand of the Mighty One and coming on the clouds of heaven.'" (Matthew 26:64)

"'Look, he is coming with the clouds,' and 'every eye will see him, even those who pierced him'; and all peoples on earth 'will mourn because of him.' So shall it be! Amen.'" (Revelation 1:7)

"He then added, 'Very truly I tell you, you will see heaven open, and the angels of God ascending and descending on the Son of Man.'" (John 1:51)

Clearly the ancient Hebrews and early church fathers believed that Jesus (Messiah) would return in a magnificent, undeniable fashion, and that it will be so huge everyone on earth will witness the Son of Man coming down from the heavens surrounded by the heavenly hosts. This moment will mark the beginning of the end of the spiritual battle that has plagued mankind from the beginning. There will be a terrible tribulation and there will be a great deception by a man known as the anti-Christ. After the 7-year tribulation, there will also be a 1,000-year period when the fallen angels and demons will be free to run wild in the streets before they are all bound and cast into the Lake of Fire for all eternity. This event is not only mentioned in the book of Revelation, it is also found in the book of Elijah, Daniel, and Enoch. Of course, there is no need to feel hopeless about such an end for those who put their trust in the Savior, the King of Kings, the Admiral of the hosts of heaven.

9.

THE ADMIRAL

In our present day, most people are well aware of what it means to be an alien. The iconic Greys from Roswell mythology have etched the image we have of aliens in our brains—those small little extraterrestrials with skinny bodies, large heads, and big black eyes. We also understand the term as it relates to those who live outside our borders because our immigration policies are a top priority to our citizens and governments. Therefore, it should be easy for us to understand that Jesus was an alien among us. After all, Jesus made some very bizarre declarations. He wasn't shy about communicating that he was not from earth, an alien among us. He made this clear to his followers and to those who sentenced him to death.

Jesus claimed he was not of this earth.

"But he continued, 'You are from below; I am from above. You are of this world; I am not of this world.'" (John 8:23)

He claimed that he would return, coming down in the sky.

"Again the high priest asked him, 'Are you the Messiah, the Son of the Blessed One?' 'I am,' said Jesus. 'And you will see the Son of Man sitting at the right hand of the Mighty One and coming on the clouds of heaven.'" (Mark 14:61-62)

"Jesus said, 'You believe because I told you I saw you under the fig tree. You will see greater things than that.' He then added, 'Very truly I tell you, you will see 'heaven open, and the angels of God ascending and descending on the Son of Man.'" (John 1:50-51)

Even Daniel, an ancient prophet, predicted the Savior's return.

"In my vision at night I looked, and there before me was one like a son of man, coming with the clouds of heaven. He approached the Ancient of Days and was led into his presence." (Daniel 7:13)

He claimed that he was the only way to God.

"Jesus answered, "I am the way and the truth and the life. No one comes to the Father except through me." (John 14:6)

He claimed that he could forgive sins.

"When Jesus saw their faith, he said to the paralyzed man, "Son, your sins are forgiven." (Mark 2:5)

He claimed that he was God.

"Jesus answered: 'Don't you know me, Philip, even after I have been among you such a long time? Anyone who has seen me has seen the Father.'" (John 14:9)

"I and the Father are one." (John 10:30)

He claimed that he was God's Son.

"Why then do you accuse me of blasphemy because I said, 'I am God's Son'? Do not believe me unless I do the works of my Father. But if I do them, even though you do not believe me, believe the works, that you may know and understand that the Father is in me, and I in the Father." (John 10:36-38)

He claimed that he would die and come back to life.

"He said to them, "The Son of Man is going to be delivered into the hands of men. They will kill him, and after three days he will rise." (Mark 9:31)

Jesus ascended into heaven.

"After the Lord Jesus had spoken to them, he was taken up into heaven and he sat at the right hand of God." (Mark 16:19-20)

"When he had led them out to the vicinity of Bethany, he lifted up his hands and blessed them. While he was blessing them, he left them and was taken up into heaven. Then they worshiped him and returned to Jerusalem with great joy." (Luke 24:50-52)

Jesus is the Commander of angels.

"Do you think I cannot call on my Father, and he will at once put at my disposal more than twelve legions of angels?" (Matthew 26:53)

"And he will send his angels and gather his elect from the four winds, from the ends of the earth to the ends of the heavens." (Mark 13:27)

Jesus will enter heaven, accompanied by angels.

"If anyone is ashamed of me and my words in this adulterous and sinful generation, the Son of Man will be ashamed of them when he comes in his Father's glory with the holy angels." (Mark 8:38)

Jesus' identity was not edited by zealous followers—they didn't need to. The Messiah's identity was detailed in Old Testament books like Isaiah and Ezekiel and Daniel. Jesus was also a key figure in the book of Enoch, quite possibly one of the oldest source books found in the Dead Sea Scrolls and a book that is apparently held in high esteem by ancient astronaut theorists. And this is a bit of a frustration to me because many of the experts in the ancient alien programs present the Book of Enoch as an excellent source of proof that UFOs existed in ancient times, which they did. Unfortunately, they do not expand their theories into the full context of the book, which is actually apocalyptic and Messianic. Why? Because it speaks of the Christ, the Son of Man, the same mentioned in the Bible. In the same way, the Messianic references in scripture point out that Jesus was with God, in heaven, from the beginning of time. Therefore, the Book of Enoch is not only an excellent source for understanding the nature of angels and the historical account of Enoch's "walk with God", it also affirms the existence and prophetic coming of the Son of Man.

"There I beheld the Ancient of Days, whose head was like wool, and with him another, whose countenance resembled that of man. His countenance was full of grace, like that of one of the holy angels. Then I inquired of one of the angels, who went with me, and who showed me every secret thing, concerning this Son of Man; who he was; whence he was and why he accompanied the Ancient of Days.

He answered and said to me, 'This is the Son of Man, to whom righteousness belongs; with whom righteousness has dwelt; and who will reveal all the treasures of that which is concealed; for the Lord of spirits has chosen him; and his portion has surpassed all before the Lord of spirits in everlasting uprightness.'" (Enoch 46: 1-2)

For those who know Christ, this is a beautiful and heartening account of the Savior. To imagine Jesus healing the blind and feeding the famished during his lifetime is one experience; to read an account of his presence in heaven in a pre-flood context is another experience altogether. And yet the passage goes on. The verse sounds a lot more like the New Testament Jesus, than the ancient alien theorist's idea of Enoch's alleged association with aliens.

"In that hour was this Son of Man invoked before the Lord of spirits, and his name in the presence of the Ancient of Days.

Before the sun and the signs were created, before the stars of heaven were formed, his name was invoked in the presence of the Lord of spirits. A support shall he be for the righteous and the holy to lean upon, without failing; and he shall be the light of nations.

He shall be the hope of those whose hearts are troubled. All, who dwell on earth, shall fall down and worship before him; shall bless and glorify him, and sing praises to the name of the Lord of spirits. Therefore the Elect and the Concealed One existed in his presence, before the World was created, and forever." (Enoch 48: 2-5)

Is this the same Messianic "Son of Man" in the Bible? He truly is. Praise God! God and his angels would address select individuals throughout scripture as "Son of Man" because that is what a man is. Angels, in many passages, are called "sons of God". The "Son of Man" used in the book of Daniel, however, is a Messianic reference that indicates both the Messiah's humanity and his eternal glory, affirming that the Messiah would be both God and man. This was a well-known fact among those who would later refer to the Messiah as the Son of Man, including Jesus who designates himself as that very person. Enoch gave a wonderful account of the Messiah, and it was written, quite possibly, long before the Masoretic Text was penned. Nothing could be more reassuring to the believer than knowing that Enoch, who is well known for his 300-year, intimate walk with God and adventures with angels in the heavens, witnessed the pre-incarnate Christ and all his glory.

"In that day shall the Most High rise up to execute the great judgment upon all sinners, and to commit the guardianship of all the righteous and holy to the holy angels, that they may protect them as the apple of an eye, until every evil and every crime be annihilated. Whether or not the righteous sleep securely, wise men shall then truly perceive. And the sons of the earth shall understand every word of that book, knowing that their riches cannot save them in the ruin of their crimes." (Enoch 99:2-4)

This Son of Man will return according to the biblical, non-biblical, and Enochial prophecy.

"Lord Kalki, the Lord of the universe, will mount His swift white horse, Devadatta and, sword in hand, travel over the earth exhibiting His eight mystic opulences and eight special qualities of Godhead. Displaying His unequaled effulgence and riding with great speed, He will kill by the millions those thieves who have dared dress as kings."[7]

"As the weeds are pulled up and burned in the fire, so it will be at the end of the age. The Son of Man will send out his angels, and they will weed out of his kingdom everything that causes sin and all who do evil." (Matt. 13:40-41)

"I saw in the night visions, and behold, with the clouds of heaven there came one like a Son of Man, and he came to the

Ancient of Days and was presented before him. And to him was given dominion and glory and a kingdom, that all peoples, nations, and languages should serve him; his dominion is an everlasting dominion, which shall not pass away, and his kingdom one that shall not be destroyed." (Daniel 7:13-14)

"And now, Father, glorify me in your presence with the glory I had with you before the world began." (John 17:5)

"When Jesus spoke again to the people, he said, 'I am the light of the world. Whoever follows me will never walk in darkness, but will have the light of life.'" (John 8:12)

Although there are too may prophecies to address in the context of this book, the following is a telling prophecy of the Christ penned long before his birth. Because Enoch was found in the Dead Sea Scrolls, the possibility that the early Church fathers adapted the Old Testament to fit their Savior is completely negated, once again showing that Jesus, the self-proclaimed Son of Man, is the same "Son of Man" mentioned in Enoch, Daniel, and Isaiah. This is more than a coincidence, and his relationship to angels is more than an accident. Although poor and born under Roman rule, there is something indisputably unique about this man who claimed to be the Admiral of God's angels. And yet it was foretold that in all his authority afforded by God, he would be punished for the sins of man, rise from the dead, and return in the clouds.

*"For He was cut off from the land of the living; For the transgressions of My people He was stricken. And they made His grave with the wicked—But with the rich at His death, Because He had done no violence, Nor was any deceit in His mouth. Yet it pleased the LORD to bruise Him; He has put Him to grief. When You make His soul an offering for sin, He shall see **His seed**, He shall prolong His days, And the pleasure of the LORD shall prosper in His hand. He shall see the labor of His soul, and be satisfied.*

By His knowledge My righteous Servant shall justify many, For He shall bear their iniquities. Therefore I will divide Him a portion with the great, And He shall divide the spoil with the strong, Because He poured out His soul unto death, And He was numbered with the transgressors, And He bore the sin of many, And made intercession for the transgressors." (Isaiah 53: 8-12 NKJV)

Jesus claimed that his very presence was a sign that the kingdom of God has come to earth. He didn't claim to be *a god*; he professed to be *The God*. His life, miracles, declarations, and the timetable of his birth declare that he is the Hebrew Messiah, thereby making him master of the angels, and linking him to the UFO Universe. And all of this we hear directly from his words. If Jesus' claims have any validity, they certainly connect him to the angels discussed in scripture and in the other books referenced such as Enoch, Jasher, Jubilees, and others. Of course, Jesus' entrance into our planet involved plenty of angels from Gabriel's proclamation of the virgin birth, to the guiding "star" over Bethlehem, to Joseph's angelic visitations and warnings. And if we look at the Book of Mary and the Infancy books detailing Mary's youth and the youth of her child, we see angels directing the steps of almost every player relating to the birth of the Savior.

Anyone who'd dare claim to be "God" today would be scorned, thrown into a psycho ward, or eventually become destitute and friendless. I mean who wants to associate with someone like that? Only crazy people talk that way and everyone recognizes them for what they are. Not so in Jesus' case. He was a game changer. He claimed to be God, and that he was not from this world. And despite those claims, he rose to prominence without military or political ambition, and everything about his message conveyed his claim to deity. His life was not about what he could do; it was about who he was, and this fact alone separates Jesus from every other flesh and blood man-made or self-proclaimed god.

His life was not about life here on earth; it was about the kingdom of heaven. His life was not about himself; it was about humanity. No matter how much skeptics try to minimize or disregard the life of Jesus, he is so unique from all other "gods" that he was either beyond insane or he was who he claimed to be. There are no other choices.

If a Jew claimed to be God in Jerusalem, 33 AD, he or she would've been considered worse than crazy; they would've been blasphemers, hated, and isolated from the Hebrew faith if they survived a stoning by the masses. But that's not what scripture tells us about this man who claimed that he was not from this earth—this alien among us. Adoring crowds, devoted followers, and close friends surrounded Jesus from the moment he began his work until he took his last breath, not because he professed to be God, but because there was strong evidence that he was the Messiah—the Son of Man. Sure there were those who questioned him, even his siblings, and those who grew up with him. But he spoke as one with authority and even today his words offer an endless amount of wisdom powerful enough to change the hardest of hearts, including my own.

Many thought he was the Messiah, and debates raged over his identity. He was loved by thousands and greeted by large crowds as he entered Jerusalem just prior to his arrest, with worshipful onlookers shouting words of adoration, *"Hosanna to the Son of David! Blessed is he who comes in the name of the Lord! Hosanna in the highest heaven!"*

Even after his death, when all seemed lost, his followers quickly changed from hopeless and defeated, to firm believers, happy to give up their lives for the glory of their risen King, the Savior. They claimed to have seen the scars on his hands and feet. He appeared to hundreds and spoke of the kingdom of heaven. And finally, they watched him ascend up into the clouds right before their very eyes.

Whoever he was, he was certainly alien to the people who he ministered to, providing them a glimpse into the kingdom of God. His persona was so extraordinary that despite the normal consequences that would've befallen a regular man of his time for making such outlandish claims about himself, his followers, many who were Jewish, took his message of hope and forgiveness to the far corners of the planet. And no matter how much they were persecuted, the message persisted, and spread throughout the earth to all who were willing to simply "believe". For that was all Jesus asks of his followers—to believe that he was the One he said he was—the Son of God. Therefore, there is only one of two conclusions that can be made about Jesus:

1. He was insane, and a deceiver of the highest order.

-or-

2. He was exactly who he said he was—God made flesh—the Son of Man.

Although it's easy to discard his claims, one simply cannot look at the evidence of Jesus' life and conclude that he was an insane, extraterrestrial, or deceitful egomaniac—the evidence is quite contrary. We all know people who are "jacked" up. We recognize when a person is delusional; their life is a far cry from what they claim. Delusional deceivers are easy to recognize; they have very few real friends; their lies are apparent, and if they are not, they are found out soon enough. Similarly, crazy people are easy to identify. Their foolishness and dementia cannot be hidden for more than a few minutes, and they certainly do not garner the praise of men.

On the other hand, we gravitate to those who are of sound mind, who are sensible, likeable and outgoing. We want to hang out with them, and we secretly want to be more like them, but we don't worship them or die for them. And when that has happened in the context of cult activity, time eventually tells the truth about the cult leader's deception.

It has been over 2,000 years since Christ started his church, and his words are as rich as they were when they were first spoken, breathing life into any soul who faithfully trusts in Him. It's not status, power, or miracles that make Jesus rise above all other spiritual leaders. It wasn't his teaching that made Jesus so unique, although his words are incredibly wise directives, sometimes putting a new spin on old sayings. And although they are proofs that he was who he claimed to be, it's not just the prophecies he fulfilled that make him unique. The thing that separates Jesus from all men of similar status was his bold claim of deity. This alien among us was not just a rock-star of his time. He did not make a small assertion. He declared that he created the very ones he came to serve, that he was the God of his accusers, and that he would return one day to judge all men, and would be seen coming down from heaven in the clouds with his angels at his side. Now, that is a pretty dramatic promise, and in stark contrast to the work of the "prince of this world".

Jesus was different—different enough to change the world, not by might or power, but by his humble and authoritative teaching, and most importantly, by his death and resurrection witnessed by hundreds (1 Corinthians 15:5-7). He did amazing things: performed healings, gave the blind sight, the deaf hearing, cast out demons, and brought the dead back to life. He taught what it means to love, and showed us how much God loves the human race by example, not just with his words, but by his actions. He befriended the friendless and encouraged the oddballs of his time. When self-righteous spiritual rulers tried to trap him, he pointed out their hypocrisy. When confronted with questions of his political ideologies, he looked to God as the ultimate authority, and made no qualms about paying taxes— *"Give to Caesar what is Caesar's,"* he said, *"but give to God what is God's"*. He was different, so different in fact that I would venture to say that he was an *alien*, not in the way we think of alien beings from outer space, but in terms of his uniqueness, his distinct claims, and in terms of the remarkable impact he made in only three years of public activity.

Jesus was an alien in this world and he made that perfectly clear by stating over and over that his kingdom was not of this earth, and that he was not concerned with the things of men. He did not come to earth to release the Jews from the tyranny of the Roman Empire; he came to free this earth from the tyranny of sin and death. He did not come to bring riches and prosperity. He came because he knew this physical world is temporal and broken, and until the spiritual battles in the heavens come to an end, creation will continue to suffer. He came because his life, death, and resurrection would permanently fix the spiritual woes of each individual. Through faith, even the worst of sinners are welcome into his eternal kingdom, and the angels in heaven sing praise to God every time one turns to the Savior. And maybe, when someone sees a hovering light in the sky, an angel is watching and waiting to report the news to the rest of the bunch when someone accepts the gospel message.

"I tell you, there is rejoicing in the presence of the angels of God over one sinner who repents." ~ Jesus (Luke 15:10)

10.

DAYS OF NOAH

"As it was in the days of Noah, so it will be at the coming of the Son of Man." (Matthew 24:37)

With the release of Russell Crowe's Noah movie, one has to ask what Jesus meant when he said, *"As it was in the days of Noah, so it will be at the coming of the Son of Man"*. As I've already pointed out, the return of Son of Man refers to the return of the risen Savior. So what happened in the days of Noah that's supposed to indicate that his return is drawing near? The answer opens an interesting and disturbing can of worms, that some believe is directly related to the UFO universe.

In the 2014 theatrical version of the *Noah* movie, the civilizations surrounding Noah were burdened by famine, starvation, murder, rape and every transgression you could imagine. But what surprised me most was that the director included the "Nephilim" in the production. I don't agree with Darren Aronofski's portrayal of these creatures as crippled stone monsters, but at least he mentioned them because they are based on a scriptural reference. Overall, I enjoyed the movie. The film was washed in grey tones, accentuating the oppressive atmosphere of that dark time. This no doubt created an accurate portrayal of ancient humanity's mood— archaic, dismal, and hopeless.

Why then did Jesus compare the day of his return with the days of Noah? What could that time possibly have in common with our modern world? I imagine his audience was familiar with those days, and it probably struck fear into their hearts because they were closer that period. To us, Noah's time seems like a fairy tale, a dream; the worst of which we've transposed into myth. To them, it was a distant nightmare, etched in their hearts from oral traditions and texts lost long ago—a time of severe misery.

Perhaps Christ's return is still thousands of years away. Perhaps it is sooner than we think. Regardless, guessing the dates of Christ's homecoming is a wasted pursuit because even Jesus didn't know when the Father would sound the alarm:

"But about that day or hour no one knows, not even the angels in heaven, nor the Son, but only the Father." (Mark 13:32)

We don't know when Jesus will return, but he gave us warnings to watch for, including Noah's storm flag in Matthew 24, and a couple other verses. Luke 21:7-28 best sums up what we can expect at that time. The omen was so distressing I can almost hear the crowds gasping as he spoke. This detailed passage outlines the coming persecutions, natural disasters, world wars, celestial anomalies, battles in Jerusalem, and the shaking of the heavenly bodies as described earlier:

"Teacher," they asked, "when will these things happen? And what will be the sign that they are about to take place?" He replied: "Watch out that you are not deceived. For many will come in my name, claiming, 'I am he,' and, 'The time is near.' Do not follow them. When you hear of wars and uprisings, do not be frightened. These things must happen first, but the end will not come right away."

Then he said to them: "Nation will rise against nation, and kingdom against kingdom. There will be great earthquakes, famines and pestilences in various places, and fearful events and great signs from heaven.

"But before all this, they will seize you and persecute you. They will hand you over to synagogues and put you in prison, and you will be brought before kings and governors, and all on account of my name. And so you will bear testimony to me. But make up your mind not to worry beforehand how you will defend yourselves. For I will give you words and wisdom that none of your adversaries will be able to resist or contradict. You will be betrayed even by parents, brothers and sisters, relatives and friends, and they will put some of you to death. Everyone will hate you because of me. But not a hair of your head will perish. Stand firm, and you will win life.

"When you see Jerusalem being surrounded by armies, you will know that its desolation is near. Then let those who are in Judea flee to the mountains, let those in the city get

out, and let those in the country not enter the city. For this is the time of punishment in fulfillment of all that has been written. How dreadful it will be in those days for pregnant women and nursing mothers! There will be great distress in the land and wrath against this people. They will fall by the sword and will be taken as prisoners to all the nations. Jerusalem will be trampled on by the Gentiles until the times of the Gentiles are fulfilled.

"There will be signs in the sun, moon and stars. On the earth, nations will be in anguish and perplexity at the roaring and tossing of the sea. People will faint from terror, apprehensive of what is coming on the world, for the heavenly bodies will be shaken. At that time they will see the Son of Man coming in a cloud with power and great glory. When these things begin to take place, stand up and lift up your heads, because your redemption is drawing near." (Luke 21:7-28)

Of course these are common themes in apocalyptic literature and movies. And there have been many people claim to be the Messianic Christ in the last 50 years, such as Jung Myung Seok, Claude Vorilhon, Inri Cristo, and David Shayler among others. But what is not commonly known is what the world was really like during the time of Noah. We know it was a time of great strife, but it is also an ambiguous time due to the lack of details given in scripture and scarce and incomplete texts.

It is assumed that Noah's contemporaries were evil dudes that murdered and lied and did evil in the sight of God—and they did—just like it says in Genesis 6. The flood story, found in hundreds of cultures all over the world in one form or another, is similar to the following passage:

"Now the earth was corrupt in God's sight and was full of violence. God saw how corrupt the earth had become, for all the people on earth had corrupted their ways. So God said to Noah, "I am going to put an end to all people, for the earth is filled with violence because of them. I am surely going to destroy both them and the earth." (Genesis 6: 11-13)

The story continues when God meets with Noah and tells him what He is about to do. Noah then proceeds to build the ark as commanded; water comes, everything is destroyed, the rainbow shines, and life begins anew.

Sound familiar?

What most people don't know is that God did not destroy His creation because men were sinning a little too much, although that certainly was part of it. You see, there was a much bigger problem. And when I say bigger, I really mean bigger as in a very large, dangerous problem. The problem is found in a little passage that is often shrugged aside because there doesn't seem to be very much support to back up the outlandish hypothesis it presents. Because the verse cites the Nephilim in the context of the deluge story, we can presume that these creatures were tied to the sin and death that ruled the earth, and that they will also be connected to the return of Christ.

"When human beings began to increase in number on the earth and daughters were born to them, the sons of God saw

that the daughters of humans were beautiful, and they married any of them they chose. Then the Lord said, 'My Spirit will not contend with humans forever, for they are mortal; their days will be a hundred and twenty years.'

*The **Nephilim** were on the earth in those days—and also afterward—when the sons of God went to the daughters of humans and had children by them. They were the **heroes of old, men of renown**."* (Genesis 6:1-4)

Talk about a passage ripe with questions and bizarre possibilities! With such massive implications, it amazes me that the author chose to limit the details. Maybe the story was so well known that reminding the reader was redundant—or terrifying? Maybe this was a part of the past that no one liked to talk about? Perhaps the period was so ancient that the details remained sketchy? We may never know, but what these three verses point out is one of antiquity's greatest mysteries. Who were the Nephilim? Who were the Giants, these heroes of old, the men of renown?

The details about such men are sketchy and mostly thought to be Fables or Myth. Stories like the Epic of Gilgamesh, an ancient Mesopotamian tale about the giant King of Uruk who sought adventure, and to discover the mysteries of eternal life, seem to have a historical connection to the giants mentioned in the Bible. Other mythical heroes such as Hercules, Prometheus and the Titans also fit into this realm of history, if we can call it that. Many of these myths revolve around struggles with the gods and terrible creatures like the Minotaur and other half-human, half-animal beasts. Not only do these tales give credence to the Nephilim and mixing of kinds as described in the Book of Enoch, they also confirm a dreadful period in history that parallels scripture because of the references to a flood story, human savagery, and the creation of man from clay, etc. These stories seem to replicate the idea that celestial beings had battled Creator God (or Zeus in the case of Greek culture) and were involved with genetic atrocities, and epic tales of mixed species and giants throughout the world.

Could the "gods" of antiquity have been the angels cast down to earth? Could their offspring, the Giants or the Nephilim, indicate what was happening all over the world, affirming the biblical account? We don't get enough details from the Bible to confirm the global extent of this phenomenon, but the apocryphal *Book of the Giants* found among the Dead Sea scrolls confirms and details stories from the Book of Enoch and that tiny mention of the Nephilim in Genesis 6:1-4. The Book of the Giants tells which of the fallen angels sired which giants and gives an account of their offspring, a riveting genealogical report.

Can you imagine the terror that would have persisted if the Nephilim continued to live hundreds of years, terrorizing the planet and its inhabitants? Is this where the world was heading? In just over a thousand years (from Adam to Noah) the earth had already been corrupted and filled with violence. This had to stop according to Genesis 6:12, and for good reason: men and beasts were destroying everything.

Let's just suppose for a moment that God didn't create the earth. And let's pretend that all of the historical accounts, myths and tales from antiquity were only literary tales to describe the troubles of daily living. Where did these writers conceive of monsters like the Cyclops, Minotaur, and Medusa? Surely they experienced enough real dangers and daily threats that there was no need to create fictional horrors. Why not just tell what they actually experienced? Perhaps the myths of antiquity were not literary writings, but rather literal accounts of a past that we'd rather forget, or that we'd rather not believe, because such a past does not suit our beliefs and longings.

All of the tales may not be true. But can they all be contrived? That seems ridiculous to me. So what if there is some truth in all, or part of the ancient accounts. In my opinion, even a hint of truth in the mythological stories sheds a glimmering light on that brief mention of the Nephilim and the giants cited in scripture. Why so brief? We may never know. Certainly debunking and skepticism make sense when separating the wheat from the chaff, but must we throw out the entire harvest of ancient literature? Must the tales of giants and absurd beasts found in every culture, on every continent be classified as fables?

The Israelites tell of battles with giant races over the course of hundreds of years, although the only biblical giants with traditional fame are Goliath, Og, the Rephaim, and a few others. Exactly how the giants outlasted the flood is debatable, so I'm going with what we do know. We know that the Canaanites, Perizzites, Amalekites, Hivites, Jebusites, Amorites, Rephaim, and others were very large; some were blood sucking, but mostly they were larger than life, fierce, angry, warriors. Because of the attempt at mixing of kinds as cited by Enoch and Genesis, we can only imagine the strange outcomes of such acts. It is theorized that this horrendous time of sin and genetic mixing is the source of mythological creatures such as the Centaur, Cerberus, Gorgon, Minotaur, Unicorn, Cyclops, and the Sphinx.

I remember talking about the Nephilim briefly in a Sunday school class many years ago, but the conversation was cut short for lack of knowledge. Fortunately, there are numerous books written about these entities, and we know more about them since I first heard about them in Sunday school.

So what were they? Why were they dangerous? And what do they have to do with the UFO universe? We'll get to that. But first we need to take a closer look at these beings and how they relate to the fallen angels.

Let's start with *what* they are.

The Nephilim are the offspring resulting from the union between the "sons of God" (Hebrew: B'nai ha Elohim) and the daughters of men. And who are the sons of God? They are angels; the same described in Job 1:6, Job 2:1, and Psalm 89:6—also using the term B'naI ha Elohim. In the context of Genesis 6:1, they are angels of the fallen variety.

Most reliable texts, including the Septuagint define Nephilim (Hebrew: HaNefilim) as "giants".[33] Other sources translate the meaning as "the violent ones" and others the "fallen ones" or "mighty ones".[34] According to the text, the children of this unholy union were a terrible and frightening cross between humans and angels. Can you imagine the results of such a child? They would retain some of the qualities afforded to the angels, but with human, flesh-and-blood mortality. Some Hebrew texts call this hybrid race the Gibborim, which simply means the mighty men or mightiest.

Finally, an acceptable explanation for all of the giants

found throughout the Old Testament. But the fact that the Nephilim were giants, is not what makes them evil. It is their fathers that were the problem. According to the book of Enoch, 200 fallen angels agreed to copulate with the daughters of men. God punished some of these angels for committing this sin. In particular, Azazel was bound in chains and thrown into a pit of jagged rocks in Beth Hadudo, a story that, in some ways, aligns with the Prometheus myth.

The book of Enoch goes into great detail about the fallen angels. Samyaza, the leader of this specific rebellion, and his cronies would commit such heinous sins against God and man that they were not only banished from Heaven, some were bound and cast into a fiery place until the Judgment.

Azazel, one of the 200, was cast into a pit called Beth HaDudo. Azazel is mentioned in the Bible, the Book of Enoch, and in the Book of the Giants (Leviticus 16:8, and Enoch 10:8-9). Azazel actually played an important role in the Festival of Yom Kippur, in which the priests sacrificed one goat to God, and another to Azazel (the scapegoat). It is thought that this is perhaps where the term scapegoat comes from. The story behind this tradition is supposedly a mirror of the Messiah's sacrifice in that the one goat is given life by the one that is sacrificed and mercilessly devoured by the demon. The slaughtered scapegoat sent to the pit (Beit HaDudo) is hung from a tree with a scarlet rope tied around its neck, and it is said that as soon as the goat is pushed over the edge, it's immediately devoured by Azazel, the fallen angel who resides there. After the goat is consumed, the scarlet rope turned white representing that the Israelites' sins were cleansed.

You may not have heard of Azazel, but his name is well entrenched in our culture. Azazel is the name of the yellow-eyed demon-man in the CW Television Network's *Supernatural* series. He is a character in Marvel comics and a villain in the X-Men series. He's a cult figure, worshiped in the many forms of Satanism, and the iconic goat-like figure that remains the common representation of the devil, his is the name of a rock band, the title of a romance novel, a cuddly cartoon in anime animation, and you can even buy little stuffed Azazel figurines in an Etsy store. Azazel and the other 200 fallen angels, led by Samyaza, not only contaminated the human race, they taught the Nephilim and their wives all that is evil.

Although the Bible tells us that the earth was corrupt and full of violence, Enoch gives us more details in chapters 7 and 8, in the Book of the Watchers

"It happened after the sons of men had multiplied in those days, that daughters were born to them, elegant and beautiful. And when the angels, the sons of heaven, beheld them, they became enamored of them, saying to each other, Come, let us select for ourselves wives from the progeny of men, and let us beget children,"(Enoch 7:1-2)

"Then they took wives, each choosing for himself; whom they began to approach, and with whom they cohabited; teaching them sorcery, incantations, and the dividing of roots and trees. And the women conceiving brought forth giants, whose stature was each three hundred cubits. These devoured all which the labor of men produced; until it became

impossible to feed them; When they turned themselves against men, in order to devour them; And began to injure birds, beasts, reptiles, and fishes, to eat their flesh one after another, and to drink their blood. Then the earth reproved the unrighteous." (Enoch 7:10-15)

"Impiety increased; fornication multiplied; and they transgressed and corrupted all their ways" (Enoch 8:2)

You may find it interesting to know that the writings from the early Mesopotamians consisted mostly of lists, and among those lists we find very specific directions for feeding the "gods", including how much food, how many servings, and what was on their menu—and it is quite sizable.[35] The kings and gods of the ancient Sumerians were called "lu-gals", which means "man-big".[36] After reading the passage from Enoch, we can see that these large men/creatures were anything but human, and there is more than adequate evidence that suggests above average humans ruled the earth in those days if you are willing to seek it out. I would guess they were more ferocious than we could imagine.

Further into Enoch we learn that the angels taught men how to make *"swords, knives, shields, breastplates, the fabrication of mirrors, and the workmanship of bracelets and ornaments, the use of paint, the beautifying of the eyebrows..."* We also learn that these angels taught magic arts, how to mix chemicals that cause abortions, and that there were vast amounts of bloodshed caused by their offspring.

In the days of Noah, the whole world became a cesspool

of genetic tampering, mixing of "kinds", murder, war and cannibalism. Now think about the world we live in—not your world, but the global condition. We live on a planet dominated by sex, sex crimes, media messages validating sexual promiscuity, we tamper with human and animal genetics, murders and war across the globe are too numerous to keep track of, governments kill and maim all who get in their way, and cannibalism is recorded before our very eyes in our world of video-on-demand technology.

Are we living in a time like the "days of Noah"? Murder, sex crimes, genetic tampering—these have all been reported by those who claim to have been abducted, as part of their experience and are all components our society. Could the similarities found in the abduction reports be pointing us back to the *Nephilim* or whatever that race of strange creatures were back then? Is the increase in UFO sightings and abduction reports connected to that corrupt race that was *on Earth in those days and also afterward*? And is it possible that the flesh and blood alien encounters reported by abductees are in fact, the Nephilim, or some form of them. After all, it is commonly reported by abductees that the small Grey aliens are a genetically altered slave race, engineered by the Tall Greys. Could these be signs that we are living in a time like the days of Noah?

Not all abductees experience such terrible crimes, but many do. Many suffer from post-traumatic stress disorder, and meet regularly with support groups. Their accounts are strangely similar to the acts committed in the days of Noah when the Nephilim were here on the Earth, and in the historical accounts presented by Jacques Vallee and other UFO researchers. Fortunately, Enoch the scribe was there, walking with God, soaring with the angels in the heavenly realms, allowing us a brief glimpse into the immense spiritual battle that took place in those days. And it is this battle that I hope to have examined, although I know that it is narrow in its focus, and cannot answer the multitude of questions that remain.

None of this is evidence that Jesus is coming soon, but they are signs worth noting—similarities between our world and Noah's world. Although there is a big difference between then and now—technology, and that the Nephilim are no longer among us.

Or are they?

The Bible tells us that they were here during the days of Noah's life and after the flood. We also see the Nephilim in the book of Numbers, which is a record of Joshua's entrance into the land of Canaan, long after the flood and just prior to Moses' death.

"The Nephilim were on the earth in those days—and also afterward." (Genesis 6:4)

Hundreds of years later, Moses sent out spies that found Nephilim in the land of Canaan:

"They said, 'The land we explored devours those living in it. All the people we saw there are of great size. We saw the Nephilim there (the descendants of Anak come from the Nephilim). We seemed like grasshoppers in our own eyes, and we looked the same to them.'" (Numbers 13:33)

We may never know what became of those nefarious beings. Did they evolve into what we consider an alien race: the Greys, Reptilians, or something else? Something worse? Whatever they were, they must have been pretty big if the Israelites thought they looked like "grasshoppers" in the eyes of the giants. That's a telling comparison, and rules out the concept that the giants were only slightly larger. But even if they were a little bigger, they were different, and the Nephilim were clearly recognizable by the Israeli spies who reported their findings. And the biblical report shows that the Nephilim, whatever they were, still existed around 1300 BC—a mere 3,300 years ago. Even today, abductees report that Larger Grey aliens stand at least seven feet tall.

~†~

The angelic connection to the UFO phenomenon and the genetic tampering associated with them leaves us with absurd possibilities and mysteries that go far beyond the scope of this book. Similarly, we may never understand what life was like in those ancient times, as long as the legends and writings of that period are commonly accepted as myth. The days before the flood represent a time of our global history that was lost beyond the scant mentions in scripture and the writings of those who lived in early Mesopotamia. And the mysteries these legends present may also have a connection to our UFO universe as some believe, but we can only speculate on those lost and wild days still unknown to us.

Thankfully, the Bible has revealed many questions that were left unknown to men for a time, and then when the time was right, the secrets were revealed. Daniel tells us that, *"there is a God who reveals mysteries"* (Daniel 2:28). The brief mention of Enoch and the Nephilim are some of those mysteries that I'd like to know more about, but they pale in comparison to the Mystery of the One that Enoch saw in heaven, and the One who would crush the serpent's head mentioned in Genesis. Who that prophesied Son of Man is, is of far greater importance than our ancient history if He is the God that He claimed to be. If nothing else, Jesus connects us to one of possibly many unearthly beings—the angels—the watchers—the Nephilim.

We know that Jesus is connected to angels, and through scripture and individual accounts we know that angels exist within our physical and supernatural realm. And we can guess that angels had a mythical and quite possibly historical past if the ancient tales and fables give us a taste of true antiquity. But even if there's only a sliver of truth in the biblical, Book of Enoch, Indian Vedics, and apocryphal accounts, we can make a connection to this God-Man and his impending return. The ancient texts connect Him with angels that have an uncanny resemblance to today's UFOs. These angels and their history, when projected over a mythological overlay, portray an ancient world that seems to come to life and makes sense of a time that is still mysterious and uncertain.

Although solving these mysteries is an impossible task, unraveling the identity of the Chosen One is paramount to the suffering abductee, the confused fan of ancient alien theories, and all of us who are drifting through life without direction, purpose, or confusion about all of this. Where are we from? Where are we going? These are some of humanity's biggest mysteries and stumbling blocks to the advancement of our race. Still, we find ourselves looking up at the starry skies for answers, just as our ancient fathers once did.

Maybe there is more than one truth. Maybe not. We can look at a mountain all day long and no matter how much we're convinced it's moving because it appears to be passing by the clouds, the truth remains: the mountain stands firm. Truth always holds fast. So when I look at the ancient tales and marvel at their connections, tolerating all of their differences, the foundation of one God and one Son stands firm, especially where cultures are indirectly associated by gods or angels. The Father/Son Lordship is confirmed in myth, in oral tradition, on papyrus, and in the oldest of writings.

Although it's exciting to unravel hidden secrets, our knowledge only serves that eureka moment, and fades as quickly as we turn back to the struggles of daily living. In the end, knowing anything about these mysteries is worthless if we are lost on a ball of dirt and water spinning haphazardly in a universe filled with random life forms and alien monsters ready to devour. To address the conundrum of meaninglessness knowledge, the Bible tells us:

"If I speak in the tongues of men or of angels, but do not have love, I am only a resounding gong or a clanging cymbal. If I have the gift of prophecy and can fathom all mysteries and all knowledge, and if I have a faith that can move mountains, but do not have love, I am nothing." (1 Corinthians 13:1)

Here again, it is not possible to know the ultimate truth about Jesus' place in the UFO universe without faith. All that I've shown in these pages is still nothing more than my opinions and theories, which may be comical or even appalling to anyone else. I guess I'll have to live with that, as will each reader. We will all have to live with our faith in theories about UFOs, aliens, angels, God and most importantly where Jesus Christ fits into the universe. For if Jesus is who he claimed to be—the Admiral of angels and the Savior of the world—we must shrug all these mysteries aside, and focus our attention and hearts on him, on his words, and on his place in the heavenly realms. For those who have dismissed and rejected Christ have been memorialized in the following verses:

"He will be a holy place; for both Israel and Judah he will be a stone that causes people to stumble and a rock that makes them fall." (Isaiah 8:14)

"The stone the builders rejected has become the cornerstone;" (Psalm 118:22)

"See, I lay a stone in Zion, a chosen and precious cornerstone, and the one who trusts in him will never be put to shame." (1 Peter 2:6)

As in the days of Peter, we put our faith in everything but God. We put our faith in money, health, occupations, family, things, and knowledge. Still this is not enough to satisfy our hunger for more—more money—more security—more things—more information. One thing is for sure, when I pass away the only thing I'll have is my soul. All the things I strive to achieve and gain in this life will only last as long as I am afforded one more breath; after that, it's all over. And although most of us don't like to think about it, this law applies to every human being and living breathing extraterrestrial. In the words of Billy Joel, "It's all about soul." And it's your soul that God is after, not just now, but for eternity. Unfortunately, we live in a broken world and we have the free will to make choices that can enslave or free our souls. The Bible is clear that there is only one way to win in the spiritual battle: give your soul to God.

The Old Testament spoke of the coming Messiah and according to the New Testament, Jesus claimed to be the One that the OT writers were waiting for, as narrow, or ludicrous as it may seem. Yet that is the foundation of his claims—they were ludicrous—they were so alien from what we expect from a Nazarene carpenter. But then again, aren't spaceships and flying balls of fire alien to our notion of reality here on earth? Haven't we learned that the possibility of intergalactic travel is just as ludicrous as biblical tales of angels, giants, global floods and the parting of seas? Yet the UFO enthusiasts, like myself, are riveted by the supernatural possibilities they present? So then what is more crazy; to put one's faith in a ball of light that appears out of thin air, or a historical figure who claimed to rule over the entities within the fiery flames?

You don't have to accept Jesus, or even believe that he existed, but if you can agree that you have ever done anything wrong (i.e. sinned against God), and you can accept that if God has made a way for forgiveness of sin, than pay attention to the following passage. This was written hundreds of years before Christ was born and reads like a movie trailer, outlining the Savior's life.

"See, my servant will act wisely; he will be raised and lifted up and highly exalted. Just as there were many who were appalled at him, his appearance was so disfigured beyond that of any human being and his form marred beyond human likeness—so he will sprinkle many nations, and kings will shut their mouths because of him. For what they were not told, they will see, and what they have not heard, they will understand.

Who has believed our message and to whom has the arm of the Lord been revealed? He grew up before him like a tender shoot, and like a root out of dry ground. He had no beauty or majesty to attract us to him, nothing in his appearance that we should desire him. He was despised and rejected by mankind, a man of suffering, and familiar with pain. Like one from whom people hide their faces he was despised, and we held him in low esteem. Surely he took up our pain and bore our suffering, yet we considered him punished by God, stricken by him, and afflicted. But he was pierced for our transgressions, he was crushed for our iniquities; the punishment that brought us peace was on him, and by his wounds we are healed.

We all, like sheep, have gone astray, each of us has turned to our own way; and the Lord has laid on him the iniquity of us all. He was oppressed and afflicted, yet he did not open his mouth; he was led like a lamb to the slaughter, and as a sheep before its shearers is silent, so he did not open his mouth. By oppression and judgment he was taken away. Yet who of his generation protested? For he was cut off from the land of the living; for the transgression of my people he was punished.

He was assigned a grave with the wicked, and with the rich in his death, though he had done no violence, nor was any deceit in his mouth. Yet it was the Lord's will to crush him and cause him to suffer, and though the Lord makes his life an offering for sin, he will see his offspring and prolong his days, and the will of the Lord will prosper in his hand. After he has suffered, he will see the light of life and be satisfied; by his knowledge my righteous servant will justify many, and he will bear their iniquities. Therefore I will give him a portion among the great, and he will divide the spoils with the strong, because he poured out his life unto death, and was numbered with the transgressors. For he bore the sin of many, and made intercession for the transgressors." (Isaiah 52:13-15, and 53:1-12)

Whoever this person was or was to become, was truly special—unique—alien to our way of thinking. I've never known anyone whose life was or is pointedly focused on dying, to literally be crushed for others. The only individual, in all of history, who has made a historic and ongoing global impact, and whose life actually parallels the above description is Jesus of Nazareth, the Son of God, a self-proclaimed Savior who died on a cross to pay for the sins of all mankind. This was truly an alien concept—yet its roots were grounded in a monotheistic religion that anticipated and eagerly awaited the Messiah—not a king—but a willing servant who would die a miserable death to cover sin once and for all. Who else has claimed to be God, yet did not seek out riches and power? Who else claimed to be God, and yet dined with the poor? Who else claimed to be God, and yet refused kingship? Who healed the sick, forgave sins, brought the dead back to life, yet with so much supernatural power at his disposal looked to the greater task of suffering on behalf of his accusers?

Only Jesus Christ fits the above description. Only Jesus appeared at the appointed time according to prophecy given by angels. Only Jesus of Nazareth was ushered into our reality by angels, ascended into the sky with angels, and has promised to return with angels. His knowledge, relationship, and authority over these strange and powerful star-like creatures is also a unique feature among the many religious prophets who have come and gone. His combined supernatural abilities, wise teaching, claim to deity, compassion, resurrection, and claim of returning in our skies among what clearly resembles the UFO phenomenon, leads me to believe that Jesus is the most unique, if not alien individual the world has ever known.

We may never understand how God works or why he allowed this Son of Man to die such a cruel death—a Roman crucifixion—a despicable punishment designed for the worst of offenders. We may never understand our UFO universe and the complexities of the vast expanse beyond our reality. But are we supposed to? If so, God will reveal the answers at the right time as He always has.

"For my thoughts are not your thoughts, neither are your ways my ways," declares the Lord. "As the heavens are higher than the earth, so are my ways higher than your ways and my thoughts higher than your thoughts." (Isaiah 55:8-9)

"The king said to Daniel, "Surely your God is the God of gods and the Lord of kings and a revealer of mysteries," (Daniel 2:47)

Although science is passionately pursuing the laws and mysteries of the cosmos, and ufologists are rigorously chasing answers to the UFO phenomenon, scientists will not reach the ends of the universe anytime soon, and ufologists will only answer one mystery at a time. Year by year we get sneak-peeks and glimpses into the secrets long hidden by a Master engineer bursting with love, wisdom, faithfulness, goodness, patience, forgiveness, mercy, and grace.

Our longings to understand the cosmos will remain unknown until he chooses to reveal His secrets, through men, or by supernatural means because He reveals all good things in *His* time. God obviously gave us enough information to understand his angels and where they fit into our vast and wondrous creation. I also believe the Bible has painted an amazing picture of Jesus and where he fits in the UFO puzzle. The pieces are many and the mysteries bewildering, but the final answer, according to this quest of mine is quite simple: Jesus is going to return with His angels in splendor and honor and glory, and He will judge the living and the dead.

Be prepared. Get to know Him before His magnificent appearance. Give your soul to the Son of God, and do not believe the lies presented by the aliens; they have done nothing but steal, kill, and destroy.

"Do not let your hearts be troubled. You believe in God; believe also in me. My Father's house has many rooms; if

that were not so, would I have told you that I am going there to prepare a place for you? And if I go and prepare a place for you, **I will come back** *and take you to be with me that you also may be where I am...* **I am the way and the truth and the life. No one comes to the Father except through me.**" (John 14:1-3, 6)

Finally, after examining the reality of the UFO phenomenon, angels, and the Son of Man presented in the Bible, I have concluded that Jesus Christ has a unique place in our UFO universe: at the right hand of God—in the center of heaven—and hopefully in the center of your heart. The Father and Son are surrounded by angels, beautiful, fiery creatures that soar through our skies battling *the rulers, the authorities, and the powers of this dark world* for the glory of God and on behalf of the world—and on *your* behalf. Jesus rules over the starry hosts and will lead them into a battle of apocalyptic proportions. According to scripture, this event will be seen by all of humanity when Jesus Christ descends *upon the clouds* to conquer the evil that's corrupted our world from the beginning of time—a spiritual deluge that will wash away sin and death forever and ever.

The return of the King is promised in ancient texts: the Book of Enoch, Old Testament writings, and straight from Jesus' mouth. It will be a dramatic, and to some, devastating ending to the world as we know it. But let us not forget that this alien among us, the Great Admiral, was with us once before. Born from humble beginnings, as prophesied. He taught us how to live, how to love, and that heaven on earth is possible if we follow His example of compassion and sacrifice. For that was His ultimate goal when He was with us—to sacrifice His life in exchange for our souls. There is nothing complicated about following Him. He simply asks us to believe that He was who He said he was—God. And in believing, one simply must recognize that out of love, God suffered the ultimate punishment for the sins of all mankind. His grace and mercy are gifts that He freely gives to every man, woman, and child.

Over 2,000 years have passed since His resurrection, and although many had believed the Messiah should have come on specific dates, those days have come and gone like the wind. Nevertheless, every day that passes brings us closer to His glorious re-appearance. Therefore, if this book gives you hope, give Him praise. If this book makes you think, seek Him with all your heart. If this book makes you angry, test your motives. If this book makes you love Jesus more, bow down and worship Him. And if this book compels you to follow Jesus, do not delay in making that choice. Time is running short... maybe not before the Son of Man returns... but in the number of days you have left to trust in Jesus before you die.

In His final words found in Revelation 22, Jesus does not summarize all of scripture, or the gospel message. And He doesn't leave his followers with a long-winded lecture about rules and self-righteous living. He simply tells us,

"I, Jesus, have sent my angel to give you this testimony for the churches. I am the Root and the Offspring of David, and the bright Morning Star... Yes, I am coming soon."

And to his credit, the response given by St. John was equally simple and appropriate...

Amen. Come, Lord Jesus.

A NOTE TO THE READER

If you finished reading this book, I want you to know something about me personally. While writing and researching this book, I took my family through hell and back. As I moved from a solid faith in Christ (a Young Adult Minister at my church) to the ancient astronaut theorist I was becoming, I became more and more dissatisfied with life, depressed, agitated, and I soon discovered that faith in aliens is the most hopeless existence one could live. Everything about them brings misery. Just ask most the folks who've experienced them first hand. I encourage you to read their stories, and then come back to this book and read it again. Whoever they are—whatever they are—as alluring as they may be—aliens truly destroy lives. And although I've never come in contact with an alien or UFO, simply digging into the evidence was enough to bring me to the lowest point of my life. I had nearly destroyed my family in the process. I'm so thankful God led me back to Christ. I'm so grateful that my wife expresses the same grace and forgiveness as her Savior. Truly Jesus is the ultimate source of mercy, grace, and forgiveness. You will be hard pressed to find those three attributes in anyone who doesn't know the Son of Man—the Messiah. If you don't know Christ in a real and personal way, I urge you to grab a Bible and start reading the New Testament, front to back. But most importantly, believe that Jesus Christ is whom He said he was—the rest will fall into place. God bless you and thank you for reading!

Jeff Bennington

PS. If you enjoyed this book, please write a review. Your support is much appreciated!

ABOUT THE AUTHOR

Jeff Bennington is the Amazon bestselling author of supernatural thrillers like REUNION, TWISTED VENGEANCE, THE SECRET IN DEFIANCE (co-authored with Patrick Bousum), and the CREEPY Series. Jeff is also the co-author of MISSION UNDER FIRE, with Rex Byers. MISSION UNDER FIRE is the true story of a mission in Haiti that went terribly wrong the night 14 missionaries fought off 6 armed gunmen with knives, coke bottles, and prayer.

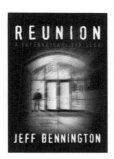 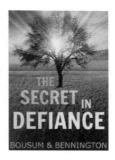 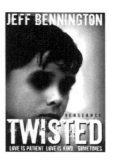

Jeff's print books are available at any online book retailer.
All of Jeff's books in eBook format, and also in audio at
iTunes, Audible.com, and Amazon.com

SOURCES

[A]* All scripture is from the NIV Bible unless otherwise noted. If you want to know more about the Great Admiral, read the word of God and see for yourself if He is still changing lives... He changed mine.

[a] "Katy Perry talks Body Image, Fame and Politics. Rolling Stone Cover story. June 22, 2011.

[b] Vallee, Jacques. 1988, 2008, *Dimensions: A casebook of Alien Contact*. Anomalist Books. New York. p. 285. ISBN 1933665289.

[1] Walden, James L., The Ultimate Alien Agenda: The Re-engineering of Human Kind. 1998. Llewellyn Publications. St. Paul, Minnesota. p. 65. ISBN 1-56718-779-x.

[2] Morneau, Roger J., *A Trip Into the Supernatural*, 1982, edited by Raymond Obomsawin, Review and Herald Pub. Association, ISBN: 978-0828001380

[3] Dimensions, p. 40.

[4] Dimensions, p. 279.

[5]www.foxnews.com/scitech/2012/06/28/one-third-americans-believe-in-ufos-survey-says/

[6] Frank Klaassen (August 2002). "John Dee's Conversations with Angels: Cabala, alchemy, and the end of nature". Canadian Journal of History.

[7] Srimad-Bhagavatam 12.2.19-20 - Hindu Vedic.

[8] Greer, Stephen, Disclosure: Military and Government Witnesses Reveal the Greatest Secrets in Modern History, 2001, Crossing point, Inc., p. 226-227. ISBN 096732819.

[9] Disclosure, p. 131.

[10] http://www.youtube.com/watch?v=uN37MlR_Vbo

[11] http://www.qtm.net/~geibdan/quote.html

[12]   http://www.davidicke.com/forum/archive/index.php/t-131941.ht

[13] Dimensions, p. 12.

[14] Titus Livius (Livy)The History of Rome, Book 21, Chapter 62. Edited by, Rev. Canon Roberts. Compiled by Tufts University, www.perseus.tufts.edu.

[15] Flavius Josephus, War of the Jews, Book VI, sect. 296, Ch. 5, par. 3, (ed. William Whiston, A.M.., Compiled by Tufts University, www.perseus.tufts.edu.

[16]http://www.educatinghumanity.com/2011/01/list-of-countries-that-have-disclosed.html

[17] The study was published [Nov. 4, 2013] in the journal Proceedings of the National Academy of Science.

[18] Dimensions, p. 268.

[19] Dimensions, p. 284.

[19b] All three quotations © Z. Sitchin, 2000. Reproduced with permission.

[20] April 24, 1978 Time Magazine article titled, "Dabbling in Exotheology".

[21] Budge, Sir E.A. Wallis, *The Babylonian Legends of Creation*, 2010, Hardpress Publishing, ISBN 1407655345, Sixth tablet: 1-20.

[22] Hamrick, Robert M. and Suzanne, *Exposing Satan's Left Behind*, 2002, second edition, Word publishing LLC, Chapter 16, Kindle edition. ISBN B0039LMRVC.

[23] Lucanio, Patrick; Gary Coville (2002). Smokin' Rockets: The Romance of technology in American Film, Radio, and Television, 1945-62. McFarland. pp. 16-17.

[24] *Report of Scientific Advisory Panel on Unidentified Flying Objects convened by Office of Scientific Intelligence*, CIA Jan. 14-18, 1953—The Durant Report of The Robertson Panel Proceedings as received by Mr. Dale Goudie via the Freedom of Information Act, 1994.

[25] aviator slang, www.tailhook.net/AVSLANG.htm

[26] Douglas, J.D., Tenney Merrill C., revised by Silva, Moises, *Zondervan Illustrated Bible Dictionary*, 1987 and 2011, Zondervan, 1987, 2011 Loc. 5227 kindle edition. ISBN 978-0-310-49235-1.

[27] Strong, James, *Strong's Greek and Hebrew Dictionary of the Bible*, 2011, Miklal Software Solutions, Inc., 1 edition. Kindle edition Location 10711. point 2428.

[27b] Budge, loc. 79.

[27c] Dimensions. p. 83.

[27d] Dimensions, p. 13.

[28] Dimensions, p. 259.

[29] Turner, Karla Ph.D with Rice, Ted., *Masquerade of Angels*, 1994, Kelt Works, ISBN 0-9640899-1-2, p. 11, 37.

[30] Wake, William, *Forbidden Books of the Original New Testament*, 2012, Amazon Digital Public Domain. ASIN B0084AIFWS. Kindle edition, location 796.

[31] Forbidden Books of the Original New Testament, location 796,

[32]   http://www.dailymail.co.uk/sciencetech/article-2506021/Flying-saucer-military-drone-Massive-rise-UFO-sightings-directly-linked-emergence-unmanned-aircraft.html#ixzz2tTGZCjC5

[33] Van Ruiten, Jacques (2000). *Primaeval History Interpreted: The Rewriting of Genesis I-II in the Book of Jubilees*. Brill. p. 189. ISBN 9789004116580)

[34] Swete, Henry Barclay, *The Old Testament in Greek according to the Septuagint; Volume 1*. 1901, Cambridge University Press. p. 9.

[35] Schneider, Tammi J. An Introduction to Ancient Mesopotamian Religion, 2011, William B. Eermans Publishing Company, Grand Rapids, Michigan. ISBN978-0-8028-2959-7, Kindle edition, location 1079.

[36] Westenholz, Aage (2002). *The Sumerian City-State:* A comparative study of six city-state cultures: an investigation conducted by the Copenhagen Polis Center", in Hansen, Morgens Herman, *Historisk-filosofiske Skrifter* (Copenhagen: C.A. Reitzels Forlag, 23-42.) (27): 34–35.

NOTES:

This section is reserved for you to take notes, jot down ideas, and collect your own evidence. Good luck with your quest!

_____

NOTES